CLEARLY MATH

GRADE 3

Written by Robyn Silbey

Illustrated by Emilie Kong

Editor: Stephanie Garcia
Copy Editors: Michael Batty, Robert Newman
Book Design: Anthony D. Paular
Graphic Artist: Daniel Willits

J331003 Clearly Math Grade 3
All rights reserved—Printed in the U.S.A.
Copyright © 2001 Judy/Instructo
A Division of Frank Schaffer Publications
23740 Hawthorne Blvd., Torrance, CA 90505

TABLE OF CONTENTS

INTRODUCTION

Clearly Math is designed to help students develop a deep understanding of basic math concepts taught in third grade. Focus areas of study complement the NCTM Principles and Standards for School Mathematics (PSSM). *Clearly Math* encourages students to think creatively and critically. Questions are provided, both in activities and on the reproducibles, that can be used as springboards for rich classroom discussions. The activities in *Clearly Math* help students apply their skills and knowledge in a variety of formats and presentations.

Clearly Math content areas of study are separated into six strands. Each strand features hands-on, minds-on concept-building activities as well as several reproducibles. As an added bonus, *Clearly Math* features a collection of *full-color transparencies* for use throughout the book. A special box near the title of the activity or on the reproducible page tells you that a transparency is recommended for best results. Place the transparency on an overhead projector and present the activity or reproducible to your students. You are all set for a successful lesson that requires little preparation time for you.

Finally, *Clearly Math* contains assessment activities that evaluate conceptual understanding. These activities, labeled Assessing Conceptual Understanding (ACU) appear in each unit and can be evaluated using the rubric below.

Clearly Math can be used all year to captivate students and enrich math instruction.

Tips for Using the Transparency Pages

These transparency pages include interdisciplinary connections and teaching aids. Here are some tips on how to use and store them:

1. The transparencies may be duplicated for use by individual students or groups of students when completing some of the activities in this book. The full-color feature of the transparencies will add interest to the activities when used on an overhead projector. The colors will become gray when photocopied, but the pages will still be usable by the students.

2. Some of the transparencies are meant to be cut apart and used as manipulatives on the overhead projector. It is recommended that you make photocopies before cutting transparencies apart, to be kept with the pieces.

3. You may wish to store your transparencies in envelopes. Add holes to the envelopes with a three-hole punch, put the pieces in the envelopes, and put the envelopes in a binder. Be sure to label each envelope.

RUBRIC FOR ASSESSING CONCEPTUAL UNDERSTANDING (ACU) ACTIVITIES

3 The child's performance or work sample shows a thorough understanding of the topic. Work is clearly explained with examples and/or words, all calculations are correct, and explanations reflect reasoning beyond the simplicity of the calculations.

2 The child's performance or work sample shows a good understanding of the topic. There may be some errors in calculations, but the work reflects a general knowledge of details and a reasonable understanding of mathematical ideas.

1 The child's performance or work sample shows a limited understanding of the topic. The written work does not reflect understanding of the problem, and examples contain errors.

0 The child's performance or work sample is too weak to evaluate or is non-existent.

NUMBER SENSE AND MONEY

Modeling Numbers with Base Ten Blocks

ACU

This activity reinforces place value and number sense concepts.

1. Have students work in pairs. Provide each pair with three number cubes and a collection of hundreds, tens, and ones blocks.

2. Player A should roll the number cubes and write any number created by the results. Player B should model the number with base ten blocks and sketch the models beneath the three-digit number. Player B should write a different number created by the same toss of the dice, and Player A should model the number and sketch the blocks.

3. Players should take turns until they have modeled all possible numbers (if all three dice show different numbers, 6 three-digit numbers can be made).

4. Pairs of students should order the numbers that they have modeled and written from least to greatest.

5. Finally, have each student write a journal entry describing what strategies he or she used to order the numbers. (Students' responses should indicate that they compared and ordered by using the number of hundreds first, then by tens if the hundreds were the same, and then by ones if hundreds and tens were the same.)

Dollars, Dimes, and Pennies

This activity helps students see the relationship between place value and money concepts.

1. Have the students work in pairs. Provide each pair with an assortment of base ten blocks including thousands, hundreds, tens, and ones. In addition, supply each pair with 10 one-dollar bills, 1 ten-dollar bill, 10 dimes, and 10 pennies in classroom money.

2. Ask one student in each pair to make a collection comprising 4 tens and 7 ones. Ask students to read the number (47).

3. Have the students' partners make different money collections. (Students' collections will vary.)

4. Ask the students how the collections are similar (they both represent 47 ones, or 4 tens and 7 ones). Help the students see the quantitative connection between ones blocks and pennies and tens blocks and dimes.

5. Repeat the procedure several times, adding hundreds (dollars). You may use an amount such as $2.19. Make sure that the students understand that two dollars correspond to two hundreds since two dollars are equivalent to 200 pennies.

6. As an extension, have the students model four-digit numbers and money amounts, such as 1,248 or $12.48, with blocks and currency.

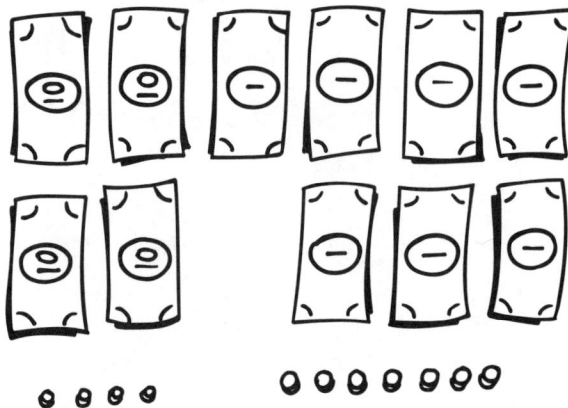

Mystery Number Game

In this game, students will use clues and number sense skills to identify a mystery number.

1. Choose a three-digit number, such as 328, and write it so that it is hidden from the students.

2. Ask a volunteer to randomly guess the number. If the guess is incorrect, tell the student whether his or her number is greater than or less than yours. For example, if the student guesses 619, you would say, "The mystery number is less than 619."

3. Ask another volunteer to guess the mystery number. If necessary, remind the students that they already know whether the number is less than or greater than the last guess.

4. Continue to ask volunteers to guess the number and respond with more "greater than" or "less than" clues until a student has correctly guessed the number.

5. Once the students have become familiar with the rules of the game and comfortable with the order of numbers, allow them to play with other students on their own.

About How Much?

Students will apply what they know about rounding to a real-life situation in this activity.

1. Display the *School Store* transparency and allow the students time to review it.

3. Ask the students to identify items that cost less than $1.00. Have the students tell how much the items cost, rounded to the nearest 10¢.

4. Next, have the students identify items that cost more than $1.00. Have the students round the amounts to the nearest dollar.

5. As a variation, pose a question such as the following: "I'm thinking of an item that costs about 40¢. What could the item be?" After a few rounds, ask volunteers to challenge classmates to identify items on the list.

Making Change

This activity provides crucial practice in making change. Once the students have mastered making change to 25¢, they can extend the activity to include larger amounts. You will need the *Hundred Chart* transparency, classroom items, a counter, and overhead coins.

1. Tag a classroom item, such as a pencil, with the price of 12¢. Tell the students to pretend that they will pay for the pencil with a quarter.

2. Display the *Hundred Chart* transparency. Have a volunteer cover the 12 with a counter and note that it represents the cost of the pencil. Circle the number 25 and explain that it represents the amount paid, 25¢. Explain that the change can be found by counting up from 12¢ to 25¢.

3. Have the students count aloud as you place three pennies (at 13¢, 14¢, and 15¢) and a dime (at 25¢) on the hundred chart. Make sure that students understand that the dime represents a jump of 10, since it is worth 10¢. The students can check their work by adding the cost of the item to the amount of change received—it should equal the amount paid.

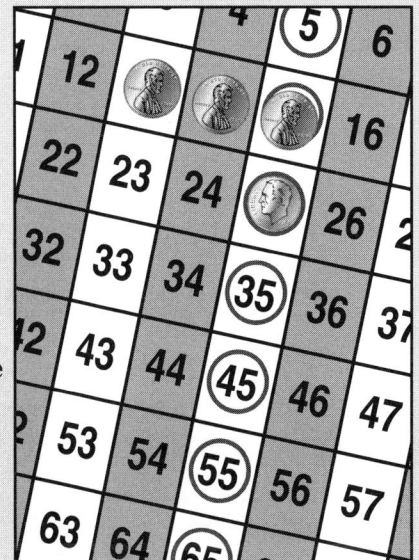

Cross-Number Puzzle

Use the clues to complete the puzzle.

Across

A. 3,000 + 400 + 90 + 8

C. 1,000 + 200 + 60 + 7

F. One hundred thirty-five

H. Four hundred fifty-six

J. 8,000 + 200 + 40 + 1

K. Eight hundred ninety-four

L. Two hundred fifty-two

N. Thirty-two

P. 4,000 + 200 + 30 + 7

R. Three hundred five

S. Nine hundred three

Down

A. Three thousand, five hundred eight

B. 9,000 + 300 + 10 + 4

D. Two thousand forty-nine

E. Seven hundred sixteen

G. 3,000 + 100 + 20 + 3

I. 5,000 + 400 + 30

K. Eighty-two

M. 5,000 + 700 + 30 + 4

O. Two thousand, five hundred ninety

P. 400 + 9

Q. 20 + 3

R. Three hundred ninety-one

Color by Sign

Write <, >, or = to complete each sentence.

Color < sections red.
Color > sections blue.
Color = sections yellow.

366	336	251	251	582	587
672	678	805	795	780	870
2,407	2,798	3,031	3,031	8,017	8,107
1,809	1,798	2,241	2,239	5,556	5,554
1,011	1,100	1,101	1,101	1,486	1,488
1,247	989	8,023	9,154	1,057	1,009
7,957	8,012	5,468	5,468	2,034	1,999

Count the red, blue, and yellow sections.

Complete the sentence with color words to make it true.

_____ sections > _____ sections > _____ sections

I'd Walk a Mile

Circle the letter below the greatest number. Write your answers in the blanks below. Find out how many steps you might take to walk a mile.

1.	347	475	743	2.	899	989	998
	M	N	O		L	M	N
3.	789	897	879	4.	123	132	231
	D	E	F		R	S	T
5.	802	798	800	6.	991	989	990
	H	I	J		U	V	W
7.	8,435	2,476	9,165	8.	5,032	4,905	2,480
	Q	R	S		A	B	C
9.	7,419	7,914	4,997	10.	6,875	5,092	6,298
	C	D	E		S	T	U
11.	8,795	8,576	8,091	12.	5,689	5,597	5,794
	V	W	X		P	Q	R
13.	4,127	4,190	4,118	14.	9,023	9,056	9,100
	H	I	J		V	W	X
15.	7,904	7,910	7,909				
	X	Y	Z				

___ ___ ___   ___ ___ ___ ___ ___ ___ ___ ___
 1   2   3   4   5   1   6   7   8   2   9

___ ___ ___ ___ ___   ___ ___ ___ ___ ___ ___ ___
10   3 11   3   2   5   6   2   9 12   3   9

___ ___ ___ ___ ___
10 13 14   4 15

J331003 Clearly Math • Grade 3

School Store Shopping

Use the *School Store* transparency. Circle the coins that you need to get change for $1.00. Write how much change you will get.

A.

eraser

_____
change

B.

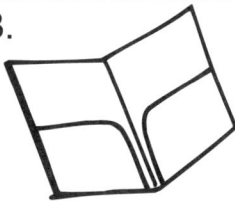 

pocket folder

_____
change

C.

scissors

_____
change

D.

lined paper

_____
change

E.

colored paper

_____
change

F. You bought an eraser. Do you have enough change to buy a pack of colored paper?

Yes   No

G. You bought scissors. Do you have enough change to buy a pocket folder?

Yes   No

J331003 Clearly Math • Grade 3

ADDITION AND SUBTRACTION

Fact Family Dominoes

Students will write and illustrate their own fact families in this activity.

1. Ask each student to write his or her own fact family by using a fact with two different addends and a sum between 12 and 18.

2. After you have checked the work, provide each student with a sheet of blank paper and a blank index card.

3. Show the students how to fold the index card in half to make a domino. Have the students draw dots to represent the amount of each of the addends. Then ask the students to glue the card onto the left side of the paper.

4. Beside the card, have the students write the fact families. Display the finished products around the room.

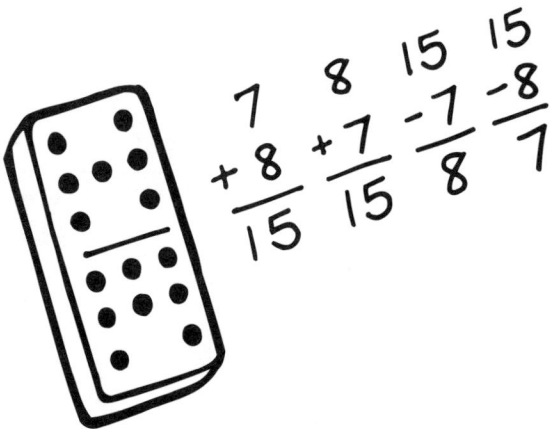

$$
\begin{array}{c}
7 \\
+8 \\
\hline 15
\end{array}
\qquad
\begin{array}{c}
8 \\
+7 \\
\hline 15
\end{array}
\qquad
\begin{array}{c}
15 \\
-7 \\
\hline 8
\end{array}
\qquad
\begin{array}{c}
15 \\
-8 \\
\hline 7
\end{array}
$$

Shopping at the School Store

Transparency 2

ACU

In this activity, students will use a store setting to reinforce estimating sums.

1. Display the *School Store* transparency. Begin by asking students to identify the items that are more than $0.50 but less than one dollar (scissors, lined paper, colored paper). Tell students that items over a half dollar round up to a value of one dollar.

2. Have students focus on the remaining items and explain that they can be rounded to the nearest dollar. Ask questions such as, "Which items round to $2.00?" "$3.00?" "$5.00?" "What is the cost of the computer diskettes, rounded to the nearest dollar?"

3. When students have firmly grasped how to round each item individually, challenge them to estimate the total cost of two items such as the spiral notebook and a pack of colored pencils. Have students write a number sentence to show their work and explain in words how they arrived at their estimates.

4. If time permits, have students use pencil and paper to find the actual total cost of the items. Ask students to compare their estimates with the actual cost and justify the reasonableness of their answers.

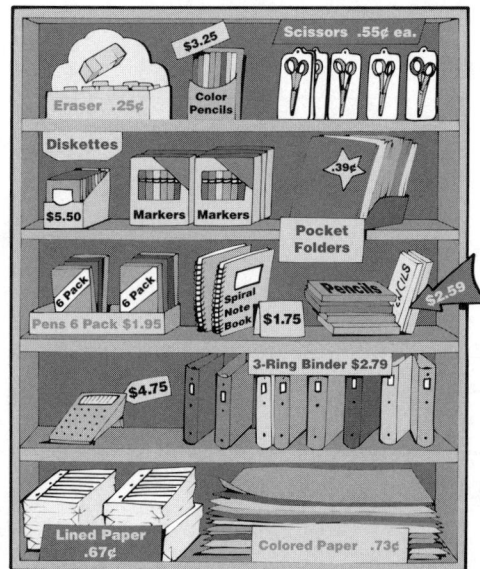

Modeling Subtraction with Base Ten Blocks

Students will make the connection between the models and algorithm when they complete this multi-sensory activity. Use the *Base Ten Models* transparency pieces to model this activity on the overhead projector.

1. Provide pairs of students with base ten hundreds, tens, and ones blocks. You may wish to make copies of the transparency page before cutting out the pieces. Have each pair make a three-digit place value mat for the blocks.

2. Write a problem such as 302 – 125 (177) on the chalkboard. Have one student in each pair model 302 with blocks while his or her partner writes the problem on a sheet of paper.

3. Have each pair of students use blocks to complete the subtraction process, swapping 10 tens for 1 hundred, then 10 ones for 1 ten. As the student regrouping the manipulatives completes each step, his or her partner should write the same step on paper.

4. Once the regrouping has been finished, the blocks are removed as the written algorithm is completed.

5. Discuss the process and results as a class. Emphasize that the work with the manipulatives simply modeled the steps in the paper/pencil process.

6. Have students in each pair switch roles and repeat the activity for 400 – 218 (182).

Problems: Write and Solve

In this activity, students will demonstrate their understanding of addition and subtraction concepts.

1. Provide each student with three number cubes. Have the students roll the cubes and record the greatest and the smallest numbers they can make with the results. For example, a roll of 2, 3, and 6 would result in 236 and 632.

2. Have each student create two word problems with the numbers: one that would need to be solved by using addition, and one in which subtraction would be necessary.

3. The students should write corresponding number sentences and solutions for each problem.

4. If time and interest permit, have the students share their problems in small groups and challenge groupmates to solve.

Estimate and Subtract

Have students work in pairs. Provide each pair with connecting cubes and a 0–9 spinner.

1. Each student in each pair should spin twice to create a two-digit number. The students should compare numbers and determine which is greater.

2. Together, students in each pair should round each number and estimate the difference.

3. The students should model the greater number with connecting cubes, then remove the smaller number to find the actual difference.

Name ____________________

Color by Sum

Add. Color.

847	850	892	902
red	orange	yellow	purple

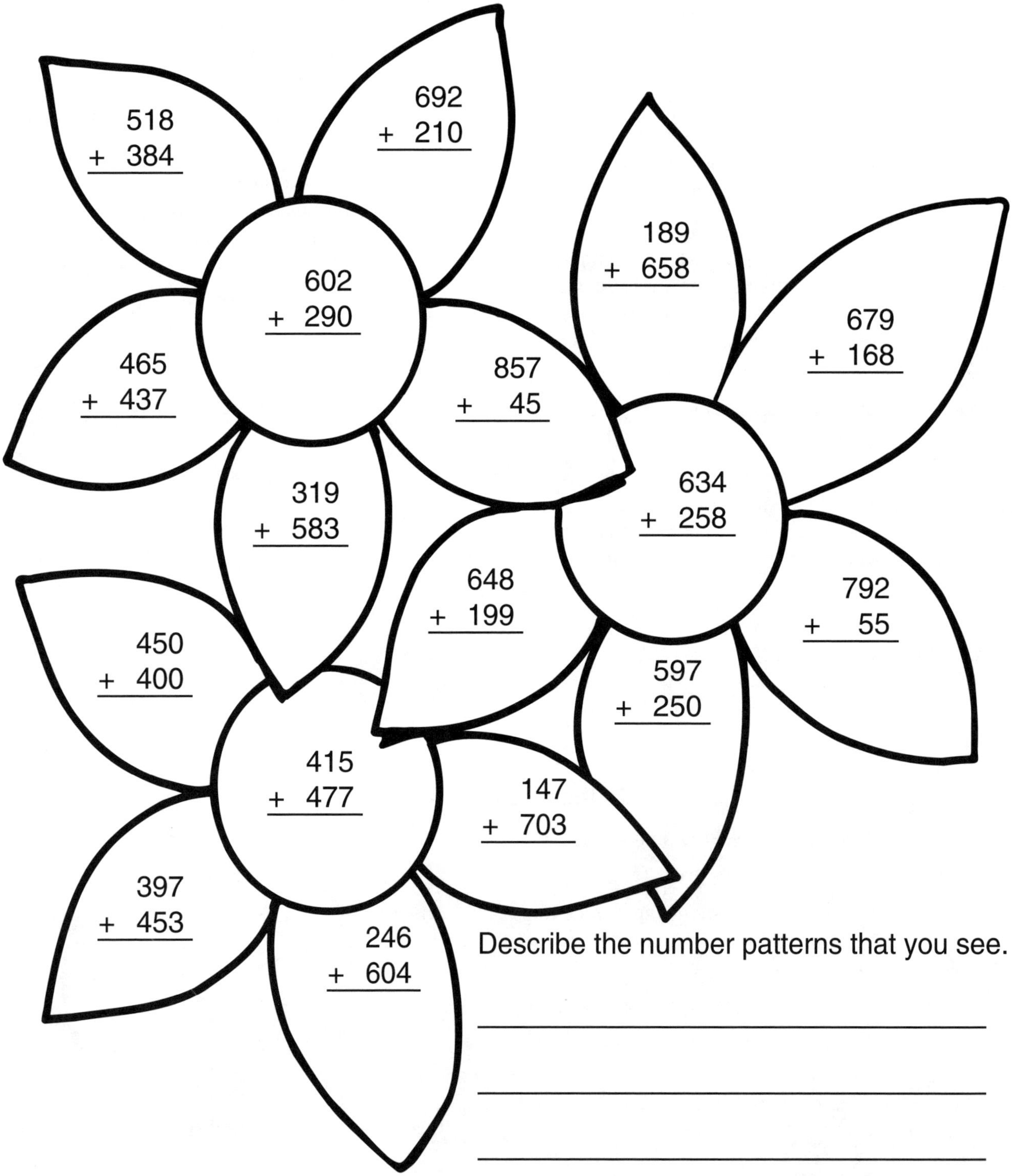
518 + 384
692 + 210
602 + 290
465 + 437
857 + 45
319 + 583
189 + 658
679 + 168
634 + 258
648 + 199
792 + 55
597 + 250
450 + 400
415 + 477
147 + 703
397 + 453
246 + 604

Describe the number patterns that you see.

____

____

____

School Store Orders

DISKETTES

Use the *School Store* transparency.
Write the amount of each item.
Then find the total cost.

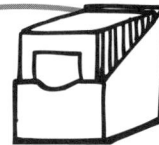

COLOR PENCILS

A. Colored paper _____

    Eraser _____

    Scissors + _____

    _____

B. Spiral notebook _____

    Lined paper _____

    Pocket folders + _____

    _____

C. Three-ring binder _____

    Markers _____

    Pens + _____

    _____

D. Calculator _____

    Pencils _____

    Pocket folders + _____

    _____

E. Computer diskettes _____

    Pocket folders _____

    Pencils _____

    Scissors + _____

    _____

F. Pens _____

    Colored pencils _____

    Markers _____

    Colored paper + _____

    _____

G. Choose three items that you would like to buy. The total cost must be less than $10.00. Write the items. Find the total cost.

_____

H. Explain how you knew that your items would cost less than $10.00.

_____

M-A-T-H-O

Subtract. Circle your answer on the M-A-T-H-O board.
Draw a line to show the winning row.

A.	986 − 342	359 − 126	481 − 236	624 − 257	541 − 281
B.	600 − 254	579 − 387	782 − 64	643 − 539	800 − 253
C.	891 − 587	761 − 58	974 − 592	851 − 399	908 − 823
D.	700 − 250	836 − 47	453 − 82	900 − 99	625 − 27

M	A	T	H	O
450	192	382	200	85
644	789	598	452	346
703	718	400	245	304
600	371	233	547	300
104	500	260	367	801

J331003 Clearly Math • Grade 3

Name _____

Difference Definitions

Subtract. Use the code to identify the words defined below.
Hint: You will not use every letter.

U.	4,687	O.	9,247	I.	7,342	I.	6,020	E.	6,431
	− 3,341		− 6,085		− 4,684		− 4,340		− 5,928

E.	5,329	A.	8,284	C.	2,500	L.	7,318	L.	7,213
	− 2,222		− 4,196		− 1,265		− 6,093		− 1,319

M.	3,162	M.	4,293	M.	6,308	N.	5,000	N.	5,214
	− 734		− 1,133		− 1,127		− 241		− 3,699

P.	4,000	R.	8,163	S.	9,318	T.	8,200	Y.	7,450
	− 2,056		− 2,418		− 2,915		− 6,143		− 4,636

One hundred years is a

__1,235__ __3,107__ __4,759__ __2,057__ __1,346__ __5,745__ __2,814__

One thousand years is a

__2,428__ __1,680__ __1,225__ __5,894__ __503__ __1,515__ __4,759__ __2,658__ __1,346__ __3,160__

J331003 Clearly Math • Grade 3

Sponge Dart Practice

Your total scores for each round of sponge dart practice are shown below. Which two different targets did you hit? In each case, one target is given. The first problem has been done for you.

A.
  3,928
$+$ 5,211
  9,139

B.
  4,929
$+$ _____
  9,928

C.
  2,387
$+$ _____
  6,171

D.
  _____
$+$ 4,999
  7,997

E.
  _____
$+$ 5,211
  8,995

F.
  4,929
$+$ _____
  8,713

Target diagram (rings):

Outer ring: 2,387 (top), 2,998 (lower left), 2,929 (lower right)

Middle ring: 3,829 (left), 3,784 (right), 3,928 (bottom)

Center: 4,999 (top), 5,211 (lower left), 4,929 (lower right)

G.
  _____
$+$ 3,928
  6,926

H.
  2,829
$+$ _____
  7,758

I.
  _____
$+$ 2,998
  6,827

J.
  _____
$+$ 3,928
  8,857

K.
  4,999
$+$ _____
  7,386

L.
  _____
$+$ 3,928
  8,927

M.
  4,929
$+$ _____
  7,316

N.
  2,998
$+$ _____
  7,927

O.
  _____
$+$ 5,211
  8,209

P.
  _____
$+$ 2,829
  8,040

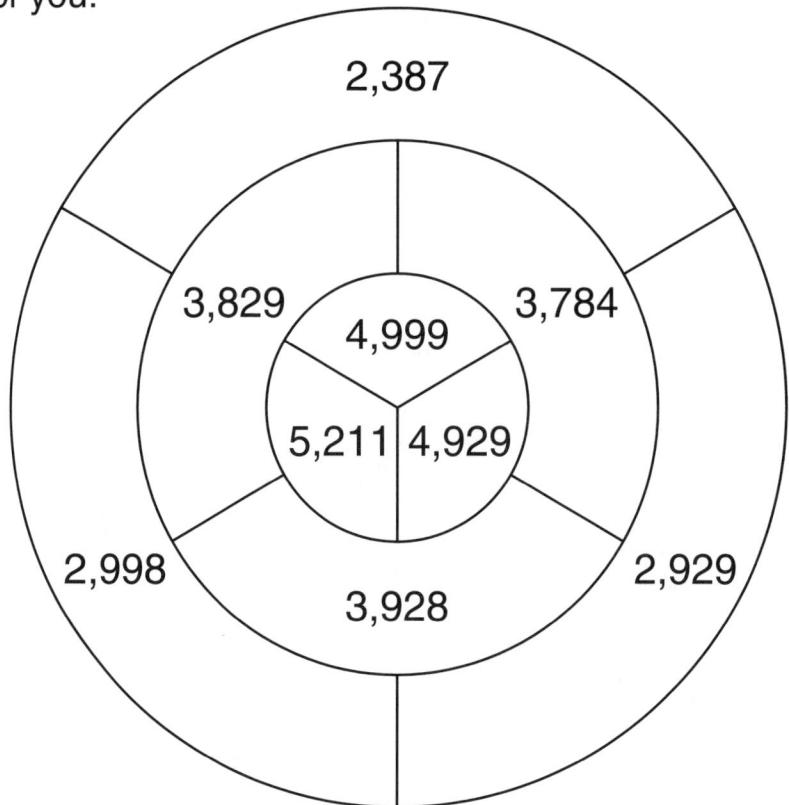

Q. Tell how you found the second target hit in Exercise N.

_____

School Friends

Use the *Our Schools* transparency. Write and solve an addition or subtraction sentence for each problem. Show your work.

A. How many more first graders attend Stone Mill than Burton?

_____

B. How many fewer third graders attend Burton than Stone Mill?

_____

C. How many students are in third, fourth, and fifth grade at Burton?

_____

D. How many students are in kindergarten and first and second grade at Stone Mill?

_____

E. The fourth grade students from Burton and Stone Mill went on a field trip together. How many students went on the field trip?

_____

F. The third grade students from Stone Mill and Burton had a field day at a neighborhood park. How many students were there?

_____

G. A local restaurant gave Burton School 500 free pizza coupons. Are there enough coupons for each student to have one? Explain.

_____

H. Stone Mill School received 800 pencils from a school supply store. Are there enough pencils for each student to have one? Explain.

_____

Multiplication Puzzles

In this activity, students will see the relationship between repeated addition, arrays, and the concept of multiplication.

1. Provide each student with a blank sheet of paper.

2. Have the students make four-piece puzzles out of the sheets by making two cuts.

3. Have the students record equivalent expressions for one multiplication fact, such as 4 x 3, on each piece as follows:

   a. A repeated addition sentence, such as 3 + 3 + 3 + 3 = 12.

   b. An array showing the addition sentence, such as 4 rows of 3.

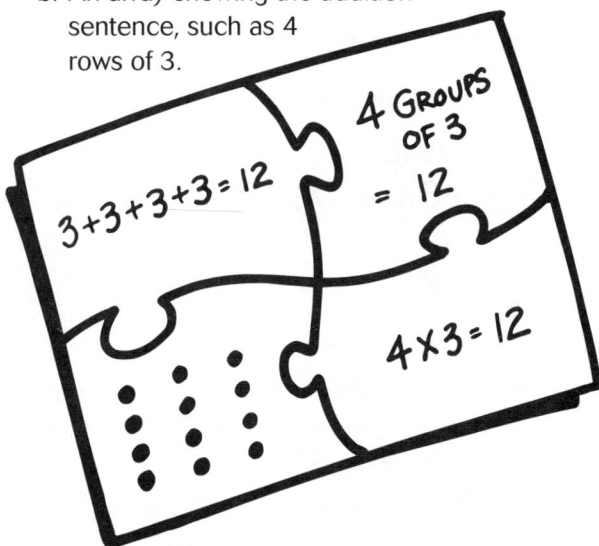

   c. A verbal description, such as "4 groups, each with 3 things, equals 12."

   d. A multiplication sentence corresponding to the addition sentence, array, and verbal description. In this case, it would be 4 x 3 = 12.

6. Have the students glue the four puzzle pieces together onto a sheet of construction paper. Display finished products around the classroom.

The Commutative Property of Multiplication

Students will use drawings to model and increase their understanding of the commutative property of multiplication.

1. Provide each student with two number cubes and blank paper.

2. Have the students roll the number cubes twice to form multiplication facts. (Note: You may wish to have students roll again if their results are 10 or greater.)

3. Have the students draw arrays showing the two factors that they rolled. For example, if a student rolled a 7 and an 8, he or she would draw 7 rows of 8 objects.

4. Along one side of the drawing, each student should write a multiplication sentence that describes his or her picture.

5. Have the students turn their papers 90° and write the "turnaround" multiplication sentence that describes the picture once it is turned (i.e., reverse the factors).

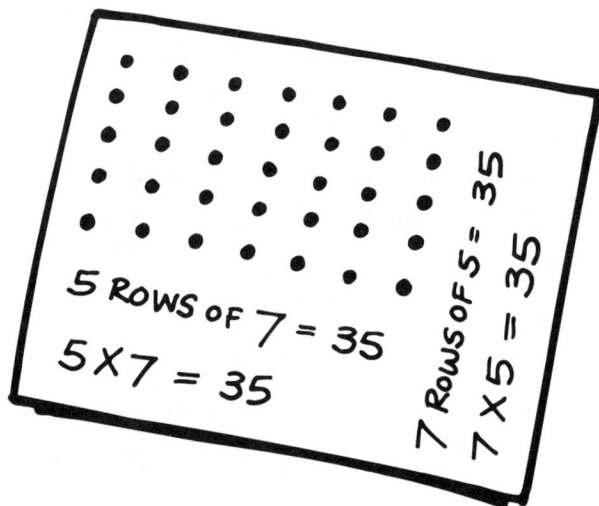

Magnificent Multiples

Transparency 1

In this activity, students will use a hundred chart to discover patterns in multiples and an alternative strategy for finding products.

1. Display the *Hundred Chart* transparency and distribute copies to the students. The students should have pencils of several different colors, such as red, green, blue, brown, and purple.

2. Have the students use red pencils to circle 2 and its multiples through 10 on their charts. Do the same on your transparency. (Students should circle 2, 4, 6, 8, and 10.) Continue through 20 (12, 14, 16, 18, 20). Ask students to describe the pattern that they see (every other number is circled).

3. Ask the students to name the seventh multiple of 2 (14). Ask the students to identify a corresponding multiplication sentence (7 x 2 = 14). Repeat the process for other multiples of 2 through 20.

4. Ask students to name the sixth multiple of 3 and identify the corresponding multiplication sentence (18; 6 x 3 = 18).

5. Repeat the process for multiples of 4, 5, 6, 7, 8, 9, and 10.

6. As an extension, you may wish to have students use their multiple charts to complete sentences such as 9 x 2 = ___ x 3 = 18 (6).

Multiplication Concentration

Students will learn multiplication facts by making and playing this game.

1. Have students work in pairs. Provide each pair with 24 index cards. Each student should make pairs of cards by writing a multiplication fact, such as 7 x 3, on one card and its product (21) on another.

2. When cards are completed, have the pairs of students shuffle and arrange the cards facedown in rows between them to form a "concentration" game board.

3. Each student in each pair takes a turn flipping over two cards. If they match, the student keeps the pair and goes again. If not, he or she flips the cards facedown again and the turn ends.

4. When all cards have been paired and the board has been cleared, players count their cards. The player in each pair with the greatest number of cards wins the round.

Flippin' Factors

Partners will write sentences and draw pictures in a game format to make this activity fun.

1. Have the students work in pairs. Provide each pair with index cards numbered 1–9. Have the students place the cards facedown. One student in each pair should pick a card and draw a picture that shows the number on the card multiplied by 2.

2. Have the student's partner write a multiplication sentence for the picture. Ask him or her to count by twos to check the product.

3. Encourage the students to repeat the activity by multiplying the numbers on the cards by 5. Have them compare patterns of products with 2 or 5 as factors.

4. If time and interest permit, students can repeat this activity with any number as the factor to be multiplied by that on the overturned card.

Multiplication Patterns

Transparency 8

This activity helps students construct the relationship between basic facts and multiplication of two- and three-digit numbers. You may wish to use copies of the *Base Ten Models* transparency for this activity.

1. Have students work in groups of three. Provide each group with a collection of hundreds, tens, and ones blocks and a number cube. Each student in each group should have only ones blocks, tens blocks, or hundreds blocks.

2. The student with the ones blocks should roll the number cube and write a multiplication expression by using the result and 2 as the other factor. If a 5 is rolled, the sentence would be 2 x 5. The student should model 2 groups of 5 ones for a product of 10 ones.

3. If a 5 is rolled, the student with the tens blocks should model 2 groups of 5 tens for a product of 10 tens, or 100.

4. If a 5 is rolled the student with hundreds blocks should model 2 groups of 5 hundreds for a product of 10 hundreds, or 1,000.

5. Encourage the groups to discuss how the three collections and resulting multiplication sentences are similar.

6. Have students switch blocks and repeat the activity several times.

Multiplication with Base Ten Blocks

Transparency 8

In this activity, students will use base ten blocks to model and solve a multiplication problem.

1. Have the students work in pairs. Provide each pair with a collection of base ten blocks and a three-section spinner labeled *2, 3,* and *4.*

2. One student in each pair should write a two-digit number between 12 and 25. The student's partner should spin the spinner to find the number of times the two-digit number will be modeled and multiplied.

3. One student should model blocks to show the problem, while the other should write the problem on paper. Students should combine ones and tens, regrouping if necessary, to create the product of the factors. The recorder writes the product.

4. Have the students in each pair switch roles and repeat the activity.

Match Game

Find each product. Match each fact on the left with one on the right that has the same factors and product. Write the letter of the matching fact. Read the letters from top to bottom to find the name for these matching sentences. The first one has been done for you.

1. 2 x 5 = _10_ _T_   A   10 x 8 = _____

2. 4 x 5 = _____ ___   A   5 x 7 = _____

3. 3 x 10 = _____ ___   C   10 x 6 = _____

4. 9 x 5 = _____ ___   D   10 x 7 = _____

5. 8 x 10 = _____ ___   F   2 x 6 = _____

6. 9 x 2 = _____ ___   N   2 x 7 = _____

7. 8 x 5 = _____ ___   N   5 x 9 = _____

8. 8 x 2 = _____ ___   O   5 x 8 = _____

9. 7 x 2 = _____ ___   R   10 x 3 = _____

10. 7 x 10 = _____ ___   R   2 x 9 = _____

11. 6 x 2 = _____ ___   S   10 x 10 = _____

12. 7 x 5 = _____ ___   T   5 x 5 = _____

13. 6 x 10 = _____ ___   T   5 x 2 = _10_

14. 5 x 5 = _____ ___   U   2 x 8 = _____

15. 10 x 10 = _____ ___   U   5 x 4 = _____

16. These pairs of multiplication sentences are called

_____

Name _____

Facts in Color

Multiply. Color.

Red	Yellow	Green	Blue
0–11	12–24	25–41	42–60

6 x 9 = ___	4 x 7 = ___	3 x 7 = ___	3 x 10 = ___	6 x 8 = ___
4 x 10 = ___	3 x 4 = ___	3 x 8 = ___	4 x 4 = ___	6 x 5 = ___
6 x 3 = ___	3 x 2 = ___	4 x 1 = ___	3 x 3 = ___	3 x 6 = ___
6 x 4 = ___	6 x 1 = ___	4 x 2 = ___	3 x 1 = ___	6 x 2 = ___
4 x 9 = ___	4 x 3 = ___	4 x 6 = ___	3 x 5 = ___	4 x 8 = ___
6 x 10 = ___	3 x 9 = ___	4 x 5 = ___	6 x 6 = ___	6 x 7 = ___

What do you notice about every blue section?

_____

True or False?

If the fact is true, write *T*. If the fact is false, write *F*. Then fix it.

A. $7 \times 3 = 21$ ____ $8 \times 5 = 41$ ____ $9 \times 3 = 27$ ____

B. $7 \times 0 = 0$ ____ $9 \times 7 = 67$ ____ $7 \times 7 = 51$ ____

C. $9 \times 2 = 19$ ____ $7 \times 2 = 14$ ____ $8 \times 2 = 17$ ____

D. $8 \times 9 = 72$ ____ $7 \times 4 = 29$ ____ $8 \times 0 = 0$ ____

E. $9 \times 6 = 53$ ____ $8 \times 10 = 80$ ____ $7 \times 5 = 37$ ____

F. $7 \times 6 = 43$ ____ $9 \times 8 = 73$ ____ $9 \times 5 = 45$ ____

G. $7 \times 7 = 47$ ____ $8 \times 7 = 57$ ____ $8 \times 4 = 33$ ____

H. $9 \times 0 = 9$ ____ $9 \times 9 = 83$ ____ $9 \times 10 = 19$ ____

I. $8 \times 8 = 64$ ____ $9 \times 4 = 36$ ____ $8 \times 3 = 23$ ____

J. $7 \times 8 = 56$ ____ $8 \times 6 = 47$ ____ $7 \times 9 = 69$ ____

Count the number of true and false statements.
Use **<, >,** or **=** to complete.

True statements_____ false statements.

Name _____

Multiplication Fact Hunt

Follow the clues. Draw arrows to show the next boxes on the path. Make sure that your arrows touch all of the boxes. The first arrow has been drawn for you.

START

Here is 72. Find the product of 4 and 8. → Here is 32. Find the product of 9 and 5.

Here is 16. Find the product of 7 and 6.

Here is 45. Find the product of 8 and 2.

Here is 42. Find the product of 3 and 9.

Here is 64. Find the product of 8 and 9.

Here is 27. Find the product of 8 and 5.

Here is 63. Find the product of 8 and 6.

Here is 30. Find the product of 8 and 8.

Here is 40. Find the product of 7 and 9.

Here is 48. Find the product of 4 and 7.

Here is 49. Find the product of 5 and 6.

Here is 28. Find the product of 9 and 9.

Here is 81. Find the product of 6 and 9.

Here is 36. Find the product of 7 and 7.

Here is 20. Find the product of 6 and 6.

Here is 54. Find the product of 5 and 4.

Playing the Beanbag Game

Use the *Beanbag Game* transparency. Write a multiplication sentence to find each score. Compare scores to tell who won each game, or write *Tie.*

A. Samantha and Kyle played a game. Samantha tossed 4 beanbags in the blue section. Kyle tossed 3 beanbags in the yellow section.

   Samantha: _____ Kyle: _____

   Who won the game? _____

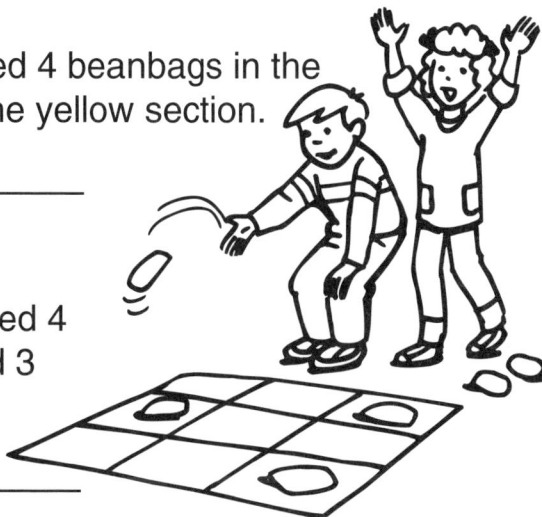

B. Ronni and Mike played a game. Ronni tossed 4 beanbags in the orange section. Mike tossed 3 beanbags in the green section.

   Ronni: _____ Mike: _____

   Who won the game? _____

C. Jessica and Adam played a game. Jessica tossed 3 beanbags in the blue section. Adam tossed 2 beanbags in the yellow section.

   Jessica: _____ Adam: _____

   Who won the game? _____

D. Ruth and Gene played a game. Ruth tossed 5 beanbags in the blue section. Gene tossed 4 beanbags in the yellow section.

   Ruth: _____ Gene: _____

   Who won the game? _____

E. Sam and Annie played a game. Sam tossed 4 beanbags in the red section. Annie tossed 5 beanbags in the yellow section.

   Sam: _____ Annie: _____

   Who won the game? _____

F. Ethel and Dave played a game. Ethel tossed 4 beanbags in the blue section. Dave tossed 3 beanbags in the orange section.

   Ethel: _____ Dave: _____

   Who won the game? _____

DIVISION

Relating Multiplication and Division

ACU

In this whole-class activity, students will model the relationship between multiplication and division.

1. Have a group of 12 students stand at the front of the room. Ask them to arrange themselves so that there are two groups of six students.

2. Ask the seated students to name a multiplication fact modeled by the students at the front of the room (2 x 6 = 12).

3. Tell the standing students to form one group again. Ask the seated students to tell how many are in the front of the room (12). Instruct the standing students to separate into two equal groups. Ask the seated students to tell how many are in each group (6).

4. Ask a volunteer to provide a division sentence that describes the arrangement of the standing students (12 ÷ 2 = 6).

5. Alter Steps 3–4 for three groups of four students (3 x 4 = 12 and 12 ÷ 4 = 3).

6. Have the students write journal entries explaining how multiplication and division are related, based on the above activity. Suggest that the students use related multiplication and division sentences to "illustrate" their explanations. (The students' entries should indicate understanding of the inverse relationship between multiplication and division. Students may say that division "undoes" multiplication; that multiplication combines same-size groups; and that division separates a larger group into smaller, same-size groups. Illustrations or number sentences should accompany explanations.)

Dividend, Divisor, Quotient

Students will learn about divisors, dividends, and quotients in this activity.

1. Have the students work in pairs. Provide each pair with 24 counters. One student in each pair should arrange the counters in equal rows and tell the number of rows and the number of counters in each row. The student's partner should write a division sentence based on the arrangement of the counters. The second student should also complete a table as shown below to identify the dividend, divisor, and quotient.

Dividend	Divisor	Quotient
24	4	6

2. Have the students in each pair switch roles and repeat the activity.

3. The activity continues until students have found all possible arrangements for 24 counters. Challenge the students to find six different division sentences. (24 ÷ 4 = 6; 24 ÷ 6 = 4; 24 ÷ 8 = 3; 24 ÷ 3 = 8; 24 ÷ 2 = 12; 24 ÷ 12 = 2.)

4. Discuss the findings as a class. Ask volunteers to give the dividend, divisor, and quotient for each division sentence that they wrote.

Using Base Ten Blocks to Divide

Students will develop their conceptual understanding of division by working through the process with base ten blocks. Use the *Base Ten Models* transparency pieces to model this activity.

1. Have the students work in pairs. Distribute base ten blocks to each. Have one student in each pair act as "builder," using the blocks, and the student's partner as "recorder," writing the process on paper.

2. To model and record 74 ÷ 3:

   a. The builder should show 7 tens and 4 ones. The recorder should write the problem.

   b. The builder should draw 3 circles to represent 3 sets.

   c. The builder should distribute 2 tens to each of 3 sets. The recorder should write *2* above the tens place of the quotient, and *6*, the product of 3 sets of 2 tens, in the tens place below the 7.

   d. The builder should regroup the last ten as 10 ones and combine them with the 4 ones for a total of 14 ones. The recorder should subtract 6 tens from 7 tens, write *1* in the tens place, and "bring down" the 4 ones to show 14.

   e. The builder should distribute 14 ones evenly to the 3 sets. The recorder should write *4* above the ones place of the quotient, and *12*, the product of 4 and 3, below the 12.

   f. The recorder should subtract and write *2* as the remainder.

   g. The builder and recorder should find a quotient of 14 with a remainder of 2, or 14 R2.

3. Have the students in each pair switch roles and repeat the process for 37 ÷ 2 (18 R1).

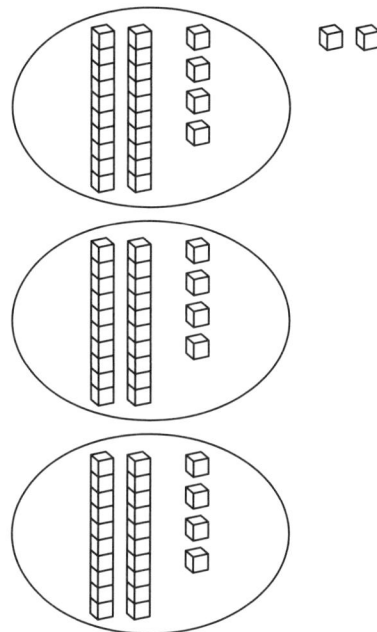

Fact Family Posters

In this activity, students' artwork will show fact families.

1. Distribute a 9" x 12" piece of lightly colored construction paper to each student.

2. Provide each student with a different set of numbers that can be used to create a basic facts fact family. One student may receive 4, 6, and 24 while another student works with 5, 8, and 40.

3. Students should draw arrays that show their families. (For 4, 6, and 24, a student might draw 4 rows of 6 stars or counters.) Beside their arrays, students should write the four facts that make up their fact families.

4. Once you have checked the accuracy of each fact family, have students make posters that show the fact family pictures and number sentences.

5. When the posters are complete, display them on a bulletin board so that students can view each other's work and practice their facts.

A True Design

Some of the division facts below are incorrect. If the fact is correct as is, color the box yellow. If the fact is incorrect, fix it and do not color it at all. The yellow boxes will create a design.

$18 \div 2 = 9$	$14 \div 2 = 7$	$16 \div 4 = 4$
$16 \div 2 = 8$	$20 \div 4 = 5$	$10 \div 2 = 5$
$8 \div 4 = 4$	$21 \div 3 = 7$	$12 \div 2 = 5$
$28 \div 4 = 8$	$32 \div 4 = 8$	$12 \div 3 = 3$
$6 \div 2 = 4$	$24 \div 4 = 6$	$4 \div 4 = 0$
$2 \div 2 = 0$	$36 \div 4 = 9$	$8 \div 2 = 6$
$24 \div 3 = 7$	$18 \div 3 = 6$	$4 \div 2 = 1$
$6 \div 3 = 3$	$12 \div 4 = 3$	$15 \div 3 = 12$
$3 \div 3 = 0$	$30 \div 3 = 10$	$9 \div 3 = 6$
$20 \div 2 = 2$	$27 \div 3 = 9$	$40 \div 4 = 12$

What pattern do the yellow sections form? _____

J331003 Clearly Math • Grade 3

Which Does Not Belong?

One dividend in each row does not belong. Cross the dividend out. Write the correct dividend beneath it. The first one has been done for you.

1	4 ÷ 4	5 ÷ 5	6 ÷ 6	~~14~~ ÷ 7 7
2	8 ÷ 4	10 ÷ 5	18 ÷ 6	14 ÷ 7
3	12 ÷ 4	10 ÷ 5	18 ÷ 6	21 ÷ 7
4	20 ÷ 4	20 ÷ 5	24 ÷ 6	28 ÷ 7
5	20 ÷ 4	20 ÷ 5	30 ÷ 6	35 ÷ 7
6	24 ÷ 4	30 ÷ 5	30 ÷ 6	42 ÷ 7
7	28 ÷ 4	35 ÷ 5	42 ÷ 6	56 ÷ 7
8	32 ÷ 4	40 ÷ 5	42 ÷ 6	56 ÷ 7
9	36 ÷ 4	40 ÷ 5	54 ÷ 6	63 ÷ 7
10	44 ÷ 4	50 ÷ 5	60 ÷ 6	70 ÷ 7

Use the Clues

Circle the letter below each correct quotient. Read the letters from top to bottom to solve the riddle:

What has 4 legs and flies?

1. When 81 is divided by me, the quotient is 9.
   Which number am I?

7	8	9
N	O	P

2. When 49 is divided by me, the quotient is 7.
   Which number am I?

6	7	8
H	I	J

3. When 64 is divided by me, the quotient is 8.
   Which number am I?

6	7	8
A	B	C

4. When 56 is divided by me, the quotient is 8.
   Which number am I?

5	6	7
L	M	N

5. When 24 is divided by me, the quotient is 3.
   Which number am I?

9	8	7
H	I	J

6. When 28 is divided by me, the quotient is 4.
   Which number am I?

9	8	7
A	B	C

7. When 48 is divided by me, the quotient is 6.
   Which number am I?

6	7	8
R	S	T

8. When 72 is divided by me, the quotient is 8.
   Which number am I?

9	8	7
A	B	C

9. When 40 is divided by me, the quotient is 5.
   Which number am I?

7	8	9
A	B	C

10. When 63 is divided by me, the quotient is 7.
    Which number am I?

7	8	9
J	K	L

11. When 35 is divided by me, the quotient is 5.
    Which number am I?

7	8	9
E	F	G

A ___ ___ ___ ___ ___ ___   ___ ___ ___ ___ ___
  1   2   3   4   5   6   7   8   9   10   11

J331003 Clearly Math • Grade 3

Name _____

Fact Families

Multiply or divide.
Then color.

6, 8, 48	5, 9, 45	4, 7, 28	7, 8, 56	9, 8, 72	6, 7, 42
Red	Orange	Yellow	Green	Blue	Purple

$4 \times 7 =$ ____	$56 \div 8 =$ ____	$6 \times 8 =$ ____	$45 \div 5 =$ ____
$6 \times 7 =$ ____	$28 \div 7 =$ ____	$48 \div 8 =$ ____	$9 \times 5 =$ ____
$72 \div 9 =$ ____	$42 \div 7 =$ ____	$28 \div 4 =$ ____	$8 \times 7 =$ ____
$56 \div 7 =$ ____	$9 \times 8 =$ ____	$7 \times 6 =$ ____	$7 \times 4 =$ ____
$5 \times 9 =$ ____	$8 \times 6 =$ ____	$72 \div 8 =$ ____	$42 \div 6 =$ ____
$45 \div 9 =$ ____	$48 \div 6 =$ ____	$7 \times 8 =$ ____	$8 \times 9 =$ ____

Write fact families for these number pairs:

8, 64	**7, 49**	**9, 81**	**6, 36**
_____	_____	_____	_____
_____	_____	_____	_____

How are these families different from those in the color table above?

_____

_____

J331003 Clearly Math • Grade 3

Division Rules!

Describe the rule in words.
Then use the rule to complete the table.

A. Rule: _____

In	5	10	15	20	25	30	35	40	45	50
Out	1	2								

B. Rule: _____

In	20	18	16	14	12	10	8	6	4	2
Out	10	9								

C. Rule: _____

In	18	15	21	9	3	30	6	12	24	27
Out	6		7		1					

D. Rule: _____

In	90	9	81	18	72	27	63	36	54	45
Out	10	1		2		3				

E. Rule: _____

In	20	40	12	32	4	24	16	36	8	28
Out		10		8	1					

F. Rule: _____

In	80	40	72	32	64	24	56	16	48	8
Out	10	5								1

J331003 Clearly Math • Grade 3

Burton School Has Class!

Who is at Burton School? Use the Burton School data from the *Our Schools* transparency. Write a number sentence and solve.

A. There are 3 kindergarten classes with the same number of students in each class. How many students are in each class?

_____

B. There are 4 first grade classes with the same number of students in each class. How many students are in each class?

_____

C. There are 3 second grade classes with the same number of students in each class. How many students are in each class?

_____

D. There are 4 fourth grade classes with the same number of students in each class. How many students are in each class?

_____

E. There are 3 third grade classes. One class has one more student than the other two classes. How many students are in each class? (Hint: Add the remainder to one of the classes.)

_____

F. There are 3 fifth grade classes. One class has one fewer student than the other two classes. How many students are in each class? (Hint: Split the remainder between two of the classes.)

_____

G. How many classes of students are there in all the grades?

_____

GEOMETRY, TIME, AND MEASUREMENT

Geometry and Measurement Glossary

ACU

In this activity, students will make their own glossaries of geometry and measurement terms for use throughout the units of study.

1. Have the students create a glossary of the terms that they learn during their geometry and measurement units. Glossaries should include definitions and illustrations.

2. Encourage the students to make their glossary entries as thorough as possible so that they can be used as reference tools in the future. Glossary terms may include, but should not be limited to, the following:

line	*line segment*
ray	*unit*
square unit	*cubic unit*
perimeter	*area*
volume	*customary system*
inch	*foot*
yard	*mile*
cup	*pint*
quart	*gallon*
ounce	*pound*
ton	*metric system*
meter	*centimeter*
kilometer	*liter*
gram	*congruent figures*
similar figures	

Congruent figures: figures that are the same size and shape.

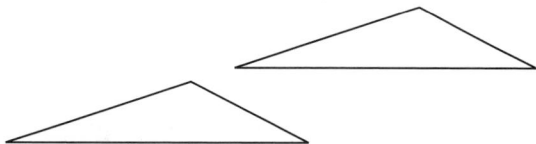

These figures are congruent.

Similar figures: figures that are the same shape, but differ in size.

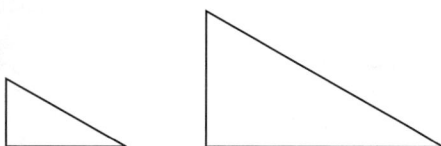

These figures are similar.

Congruent and Similar Object Hunt

In this short activity, students will visually explore the classroom for examples of congruent and similar figures.

1. Provide the students with blank sheets of paper.

2. Tell them that they will have a five-minute time limit and should jot down any and all examples of congruent or similar figures that they see in the classroom. Congruent examples may include textbooks, chalkboard erasers, rulers, and markers. Similar examples may include paper clips, desk chairs, and index cards.

3. After five minutes, have the students compare their lists in small groups. Encourage them to verify their hunches if necessary by comparing or measuring the figures.

4. If time and interest permit, have the students share results as a class. Make sure that the students understand that all congruent figures are also similar, but similar figures are not all congruent.

Beanbag Game Areas

In this activity, students will find the areas of the regions in the *Beanbag Game* transparency.

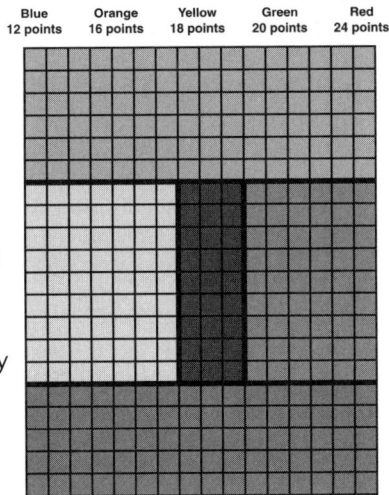

Blue 12 points	Orange 16 points	Yellow 18 points	Green 20 points	Red 24 points

1. Display the *Beanbag Game* transparency. Have the students identify the shape of the colored sections (rectangle).

2. Ask the students how they might find the area of each colored section. Students may suggest counting the number of rows, the number in each row, and finding the product of the two amounts, or they may simply say that they can count the square units.

3. Invite the students to find the area of the blue region with any method that they like. (96 square units.) Make sure that students understand that the area is in square units, since each countable unit is in the shape of a square.

4. Have the students repeat the process to find the areas of the other colored sections. Allow students to use various solution strategies.

5. When the students have found and shared the areas, ask them to tell which strategy they found easiest to use (most will choose multiplying rows times columns, or length times width).

Nearest Inch Measurements

In this activity, students will estimate lengths of classroom objects.

1. Pass out an inch ruler to each student. Ask the students to identify the inch marks. Then ask volunteers to show where the ½-inch, ¼-inch, and ¾-inch marks are located.

2. Draw a line 3¾ inches long on the board. Ask the student volunteers to come up with their rulers and tell whether they think the line is closer to 3 inches or 4 inches long (4 inches). Repeat the procedure, drawing and having students estimate lengths such as 1¼ inches, 2¾ inches, and 5¼ inches.

3. Draw a line 2½ inches long. Tell the students that just as in other estimated amounts, ½-inch measures are estimated up to the next whole inch amounts.

4. Have students measure several objects in or around their desks, measuring each to the nearest whole inch. Allow the students time to share the objects that they measured with each other and compare estimated measurements.

Tangram Fun

This activity reinforces students' knowledge of geometry terms and vocabulary.

1. Display the *Tangram* transparency. Ask the students to identify the shape of each lettered figure. (A, C, D, F, and G are triangles; B is a parallelogram; E is a square.)

2. Ask the students to name any figures in the tangram that are congruent to each other. (A and F are congruent; D and G are congruent.)

3. Ask the students to name any figures in the tangram that are similar to each other. (A is similar to C, D, and G. C is similar to A, D, F, and G. D is similar to C, A, and F.)

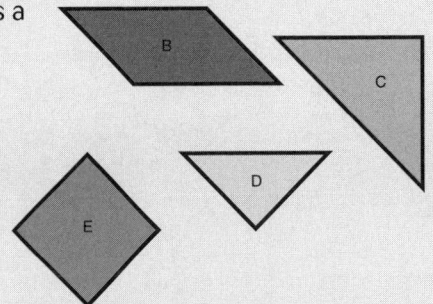

Exploring Volume

This hands-on activity develops spatial skills and conceptual understanding of volume.

1. Have students work in small groups. Provide each group with two boxes—one tall and narrow, one short and wide. Ask the students to predict which box holds more or has a greater volume. Allow the students time to discuss their ideas and justify their predictions.

2. Once the groups have made their predictions, provide them with base ten unit blocks. Instruct students to fill each box with blocks, then pour them out and count.

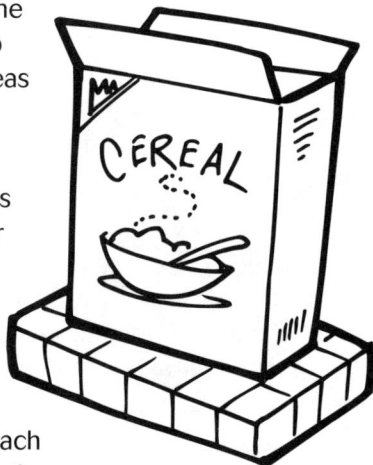

3. Have students compare the number of cubic units required to fill the boxes. Help students understand that the box that can hold the greater number of cubic units has the greater volume. (You may wish to explain that volume is measured in cubes, or cubic units, because it has three dimensions: length, height, and width.)

4. Have student groups exchange boxes and repeat the activity. This time, have students discuss whether their predictions were better and, if so, why.

Estimating Lengths

Students will create their own images of measurement units in this exploratory activity.

1. Remind the students that inches, feet, and yards are used to measure shorter lengths, while miles are generally used to measure longer distances.

2. Show the students an inch ruler and a yardstick. Display a paper clip and tell students that its length is about 1 inch. While the measurement tools are visible, ask the students to find three objects whose measurements are about 1 inch, 1 foot, and 1 yard long, respectively.

3. Allow the students time to check their estimates with the measurement tools. Ask them to tell how they might determine which tool to use to measure the length of an object. (Students may say that short objects should be measured in inches, and longer objects in feet or yards.)

Water Play

Students will enjoy learning about customary units of capacity as they complete this activity. If water is unavailable, rice can be substituted.

1. Have students work in small groups. Provide each group with cup, pint, quart, and gallon containers, as well as enough water (or rice) to fill the gallon container.

2. Pose the following problem to the students: "You have one gallon of water (rice). Your task is to find out how many of the smaller containers equal one gallon. You must also order the containers from least to greatest in capacity."

3. Allow ample time for exploration. When student groups have completed the task, invite the class to compare strategies and results. In the event of disagreement, have student groups demonstrate their procedures to justify their results.

4. As a class, summarize the activity. Students should find that there are 4 quarts, 8 pints, or 16 cups to a gallon.

5. You may wish to extend the activity by having the students find the number of pints in a quart, cups in a pint, cups in a quart, and so forth.

Inching Along

Use your inch ruler to measure each line segment. Find the perimeter, or distance around, each figure.

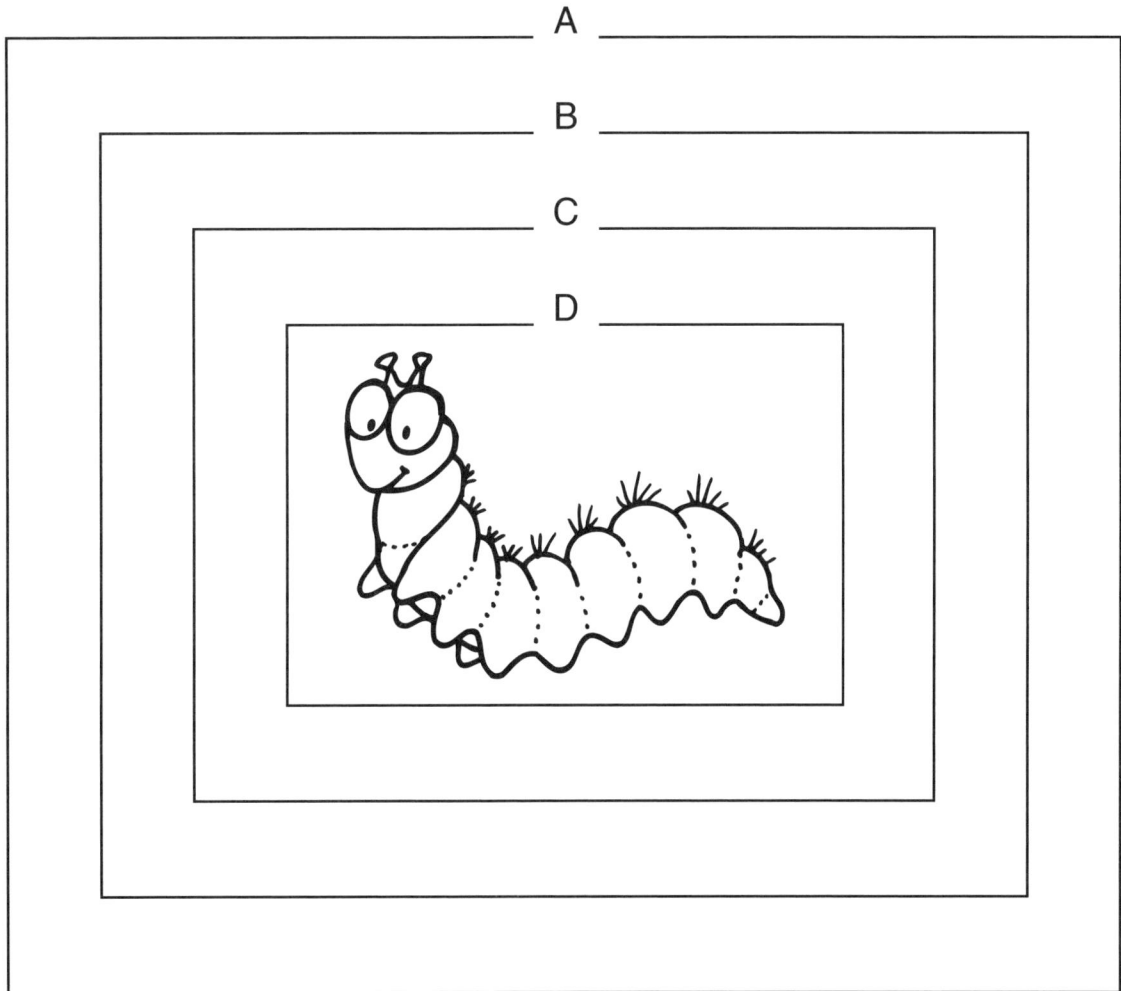

A. Perimeter = _____ inches   B. Perimeter = _____ inches

C. Perimeter = _____ inches   D. Perimeter = _____ inches

E. Draw a rectangle that has a perimeter of 14 inches. Write the length and width. You may use the space on the back of this page.

Colored Pencils

Measure each colored pencil to the nearest centimeter. Color the pencils.

A.    About _____ cm

B.    About _____ cm

C.    About _____ cm

D. 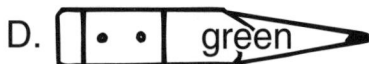   About _____ cm

E.    About _____ cm

F. 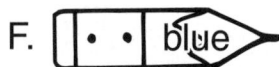   About _____ cm

G.    About _____ cm

H. Draw a line about 7 cm long.

I. Which colored pencil is closest in length to the line that you drew?

_____

Room to Spare

Find the area of each room.
Use your answers to solve the riddle:

What is the most difficult key to turn?

Remember:
Area = length x width

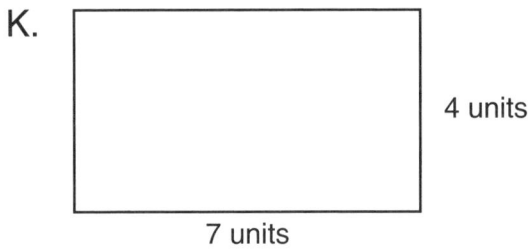

K.

4 units

7 units

Area = _____ square units

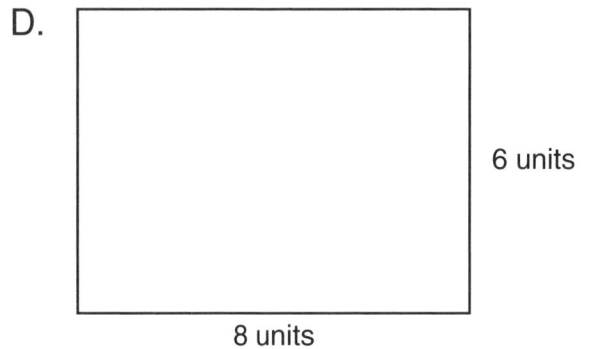

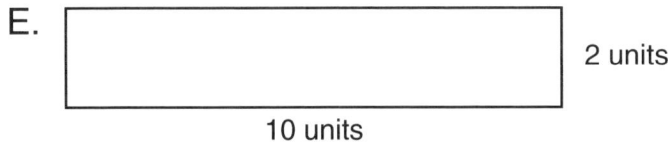

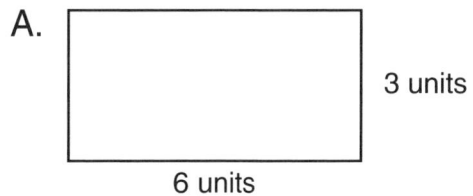

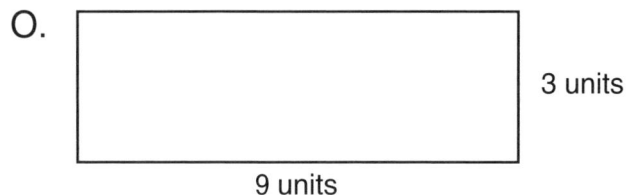

D.

6 units

8 units

Area = _____ square units

E.

2 units

10 units

Area = _____ square units

A.

3 units

6 units

Area = _____ square units

N.

4 units

6 units

Area = _____ square units

O.

3 units

9 units

Area = _____ square units

Y.

4 units

20 units

Area = _____ square units

___   ___ ___ ___ ___ ___ ___
18   48   27   24   28   20   80

A Timely Riddle

Write the time on the blank under each clock.
Hint: You will not use every letter, and you may use some more than once.

C. _____ E. _____ F. _____ H. _____

I. _____ K. _____ L. _____ M. _____

O. _____ S. _____ T. _____ X. _____

Write the letters from above that go with the times to solve the riddle:

What time is it when the clock strikes 13?

___ ___ ___ ___   ___ ___   ___ ___ ___
12:12 3:21 4:13 8:42   12:12 6:48   10:23 3:21 9:39

___ ___ ___   ___ ___ ___ ___ ___
12:12 9:02 8:42   11:09 2:34 6:48 11:09 3:58

Planning Ahead

Draw the hands on the clocks and write the time to answer each question.

1. Stacy takes a 2-hour dance class every Saturday morning. The class ends at 11:00. At what time does it start?

_____

2. Todd's football game lasts 3 hours. If it ends at 4:30, at what time does it begin?

_____

3. Sam must arrive at trombone practice at 6:30. It takes him 15 minutes to get there. At what time should he leave home?

_____

4. Mitchell is going to the library on the way home from school. He needs to be home by 4:00 and the library is 20 minutes away. At what time does Mitchell need to leave the library?

_____

5. Dara and Howard are going to a movie that begins at 4:30. The movie theatre is $\frac{1}{2}$ hour away. At what time do they need to leave to get to the theatre on time?

_____

6. It takes Mallory 45 minutes to get ready for school. If she needs to leave for school at 8:15, at what time does she need to start getting ready?

_____

FRACTIONS AND DECIMALS

Fractional Parts of Regions

Transparency 7

In this activity, students will develop conceptual understanding of fractional parts.

1. Display the *Fraction Circles* transparency. Ask the students which color fraction circle shows fourths (green). Ask them to tell how they know (four pieces make a whole, so each piece is one fourth).

2. Work similarly through the other fraction circle pieces on the transparency. Continue until the students know how to name each fraction piece.

3. Next, write a fraction such as $2/3$ on the chalkboard. Invite the students to tell how $2/3$ can be identified on the transparency. Then ask a volunteer to come to the front of the room and mark $2/3$ of the correct circle. Discuss results. The students should say that they chose the circle with 3 sections since it shows thirds, and that 2 of the 3 pieces, or $2/3$, should have been marked.

4. Repeat for other fractional parts such as $1/2$, $3/4$, and $3/8$.

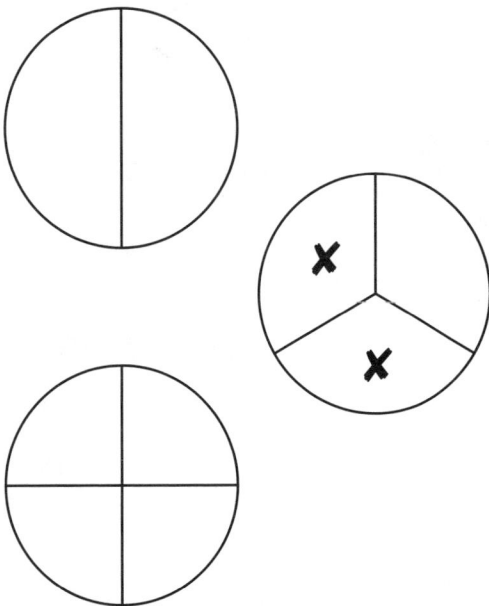

Tangram Tangler

Transparency 5

Students will apply what they know about fractional parts to solve these puzzles.

1. Have students work in groups of four. Supply each student with one copy of the *Tangram* transparency. Have the students cut out the tangram pieces and place them in one large pile for their group's use.

2. Direct each group to place D pieces on top of a C piece until the C piece is covered exactly and completely. Ask the students how many D pieces are needed to make a C piece (2). Ask the students what fractional part of the C piece the D piece represents ($1/2$). Discuss responses. Students should be able to explain that two D pieces make a C piece, so D = $1/2$ of C.

3. Have student groups repeat the procedure to answer the following questions:

   What is the the relationship between

G and B?	D and E?	G and A?
D and F?	C and A?	

   (G = $1/2$ B; D = $1/2$ E; G = $1/4$ A; D = $1/4$ F; C = $1/2$ A)

4. Have the students each use one completed example and trace the pieces onto a sheet of construction paper. Beneath their sheets, have the students describe what their pieces show and explain how their descriptions make sense.

Variation: You may wish to display the tangram pieces on the overhead projector and complete this activity in a whole-class setting.

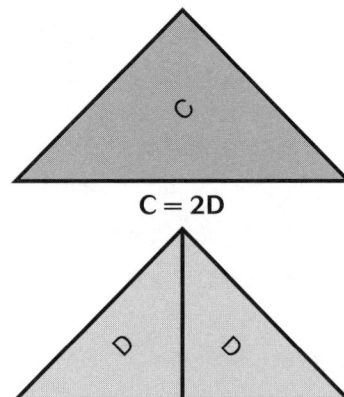

C = 2D

Using Fraction Circles to Find Equivalent Fractions

In this activity, students will manipulate fraction circle pieces to explore the concept of equivalence.

1. Display cut-out fraction circle pieces from the *Fraction Circles* transparency. Have the students identify the fractional parts represented by each fraction circle.

2. Ask a volunteer to remove all the pieces except for one $\frac{1}{2}$ fraction piece. Ask another volunteer to cover the $\frac{1}{2}$ piece with $\frac{1}{4}$ pieces.

3. Ask the students how many $\frac{1}{4}$ pieces were needed (2). Write $\frac{1}{2} = \frac{2}{4}$ on the overhead beneath the fraction circles. Ask the students to read the equation and explain how it represents, or describes, the fraction circle pieces (one $\frac{1}{2}$ piece is equal to two $\frac{1}{4}$ pieces).

4. Repeat the process, having volunteers find the number of $\frac{1}{8}$ pieces required to cover the $\frac{1}{2}$ piece (4). Have the students try to guess the equivalence ($\frac{1}{2} = \frac{4}{8}$).

5. Continue as time permits, involving fractions of other sizes. For example, you may have students find that $\frac{1}{4} = \frac{2}{8}$, $\frac{2}{4} = \frac{4}{8}$, and $\frac{3}{4} = \frac{6}{8}$.

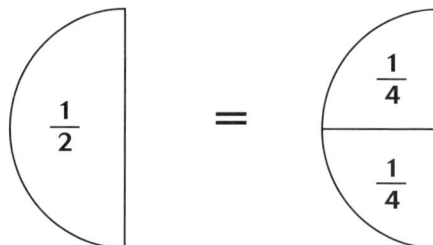

Relating Decimals to Fractions

Students will use base ten blocks to explore the relationship between decimal and common fractions.

1. Provide small groups of students with a collection of base ten blocks, or copies of the *Base Ten Models* transparency. Display the base ten "flat" from the transparency on the overhead projector and tell the students that it represents one whole.

2. Display a "long" on the overhead projector. Ask the students to discuss in small groups what part of the whole the block represents ($\frac{1}{10}$). If necessary, suggest that they use the longs to construct a flat, then use what they know about fractions to determine the part represented by one long.

3. Write *0.3* on the overhead projector and ask a volunteer to come to the front of the room and model the number with blocks. Ask the students to name the fractional part of the whole represented by the blocks ($\frac{3}{10}$). Have a volunteer write the fraction beside the decimal.

4. Repeat the procedure for 0.7.

5. Ask the students to use blocks to model 0.5 and to sketch the model.
   Have them write a decimal and two common fractions that can be used to represent the model. Ask each student to write a sentence or two explaining his or her picture and the values that he or she has recorded. (Students should draw pictures showing $\frac{5}{10}$ and write the fractions $\frac{5}{10}$ and $\frac{1}{2}$. Students should explain that 0.5, $\frac{5}{10}$, and $\frac{1}{2}$ are all equivalent because they are all names for the same value or amount.)

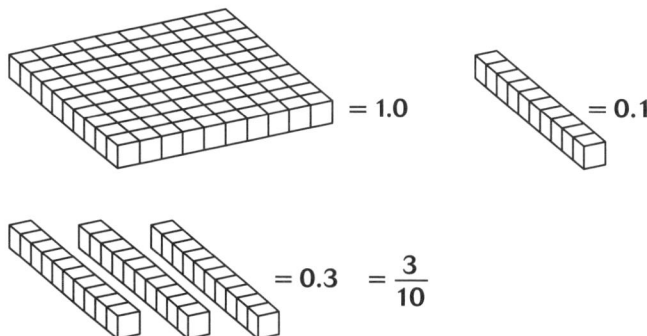

Color by Equivalence

Color fractions equivalent to $\frac{1}{2}$ blue, $\frac{1}{3}$ yellow, $\frac{1}{4}$ green, and $\frac{2}{3}$ red.

Use the *fraction circles* to help you.

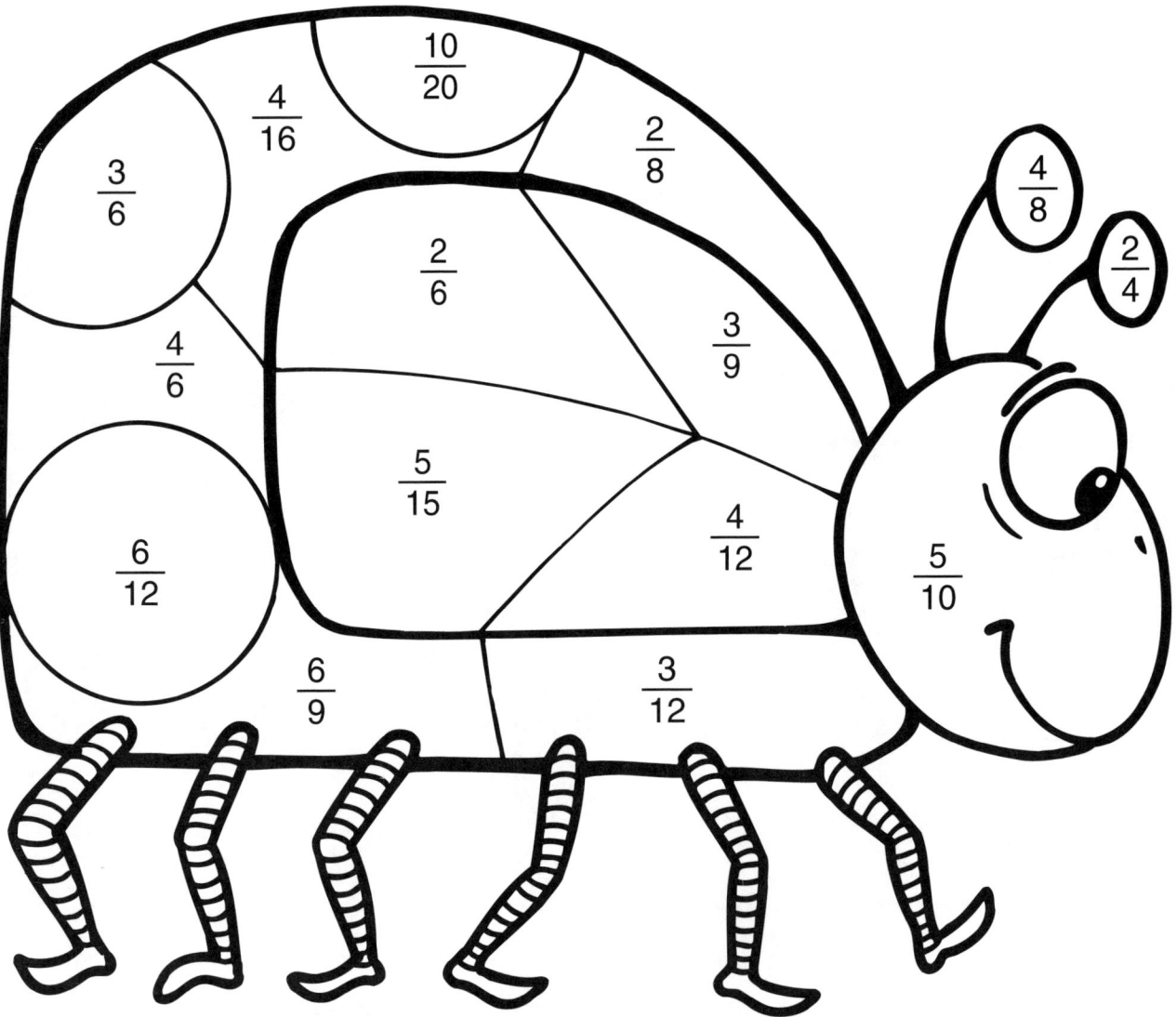

Write all of the fractions equivalent to $\frac{1}{2}$. What pattern do you see in the numerators and denominators?

_____

_____

J331003 Clearly Math • Grade 3

Fraction Lineup

Circle the letter below the greatest fraction. Use the number line to help.

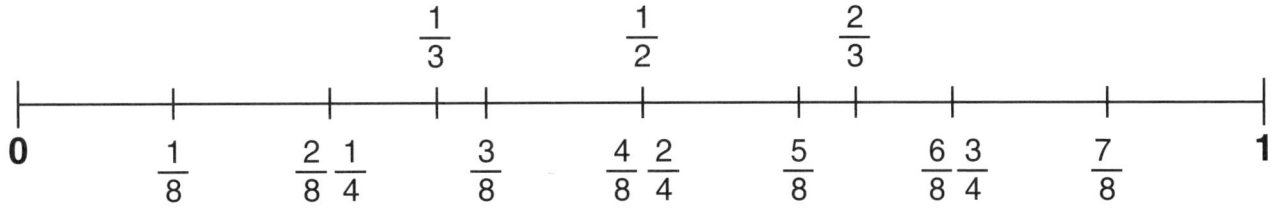

$$\frac{1}{3} \qquad \frac{1}{2} \qquad \frac{2}{3}$$

0 ———————————————————————————————————— 1

$\frac{1}{8}$ $\frac{2}{8}$ $\frac{1}{4}$ $\frac{3}{8}$ $\frac{4}{8}$ $\frac{2}{4}$ $\frac{5}{8}$ $\frac{6}{8}$ $\frac{3}{4}$ $\frac{7}{8}$

1.	$\frac{1}{2}$	$\frac{1}{3}$	$\frac{1}{4}$		2.	$\frac{1}{4}$	$\frac{2}{4}$	$\frac{3}{4}$
	T	U	V			F	G	H
3.	$\frac{1}{4}$	$\frac{1}{2}$	$\frac{1}{8}$		4.	$\frac{1}{8}$	$\frac{2}{8}$	$\frac{3}{8}$
	D	E	F			W	X	Y
5.	$\frac{5}{8}$	$\frac{3}{8}$	$\frac{1}{8}$		6.	$\frac{1}{4}$	$\frac{3}{4}$	$\frac{2}{4}$
	N	O	P			U	V	W
7.	$\frac{2}{8}$	$\frac{2}{4}$	$\frac{2}{3}$		8.	$\frac{3}{8}$	$\frac{5}{8}$	$\frac{7}{8}$
	P	Q	R			Q	R	S
9.	$\frac{2}{3}$	$\frac{1}{2}$	$\frac{1}{3}$					
	O	P	Q					

Write each circled letter that goes with each problem number below to solve the riddle:

Why can't hurricanes get along?

___ ___ ___ ___   ___ ___ ___ ___ ___   ___ ___ ___
 1   2   3   4   5   3   6   3   7   8   3   3

___ ___ ___   ___ ___   ___ ___ ___
 3   4   3   1   9   3   4   3

All Mixed Up

Color to show the whole number and the fractional part. Then write the mixed number.

D. $2 + \dfrac{3}{4}$ 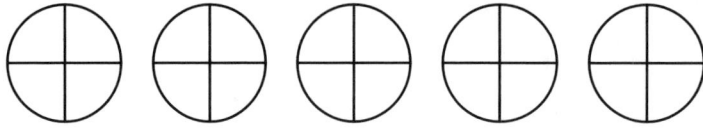 _____

F. $4 + \dfrac{1}{2}$ 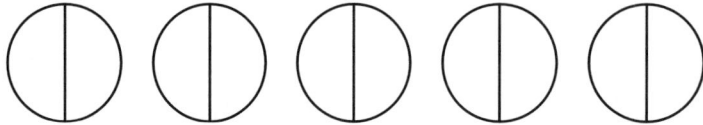 _____

B. $1 + \dfrac{1}{2}$ 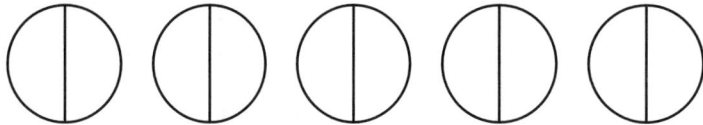 _____

C. $2 + \dfrac{1}{4}$  _____

E. $3 + \dfrac{1}{2}$ 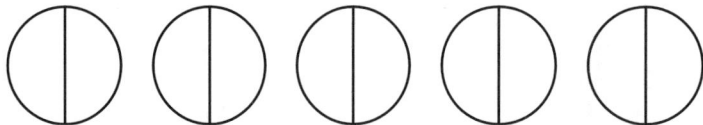 _____

A. $1 + \dfrac{1}{4}$  _____

Draw and label the points on the number line. Order the numbers from least to greatest.

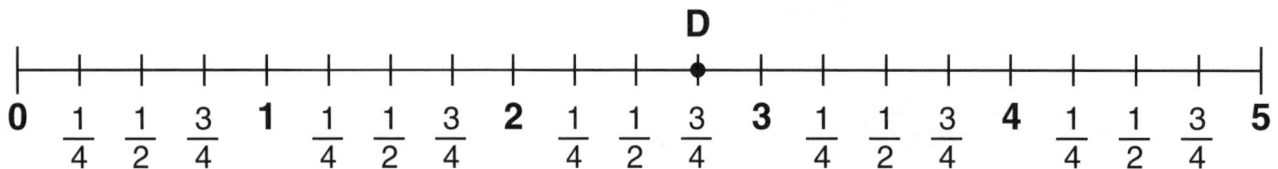

What pattern do you notice? _____

Play Decimal B-I-N-G-O

Write the decimal. Circle your answer on the B-I-N-G-O board.
Draw a line through the winning row.

A. Three and four tenths _____	B. Four and two tenths _____
C. Five and seventeen hundredths _____	D. Two and forty-five hundredths _____
E. Nine and three tenths _____	F. Ten and two tenths _____
G. One and fourteen hundredths _____	H. Five and six tenths _____
I. Two and seven tenths _____	J. Three and fifty-nine hundredths _____
K. Four and eighty-six hundredths _____	L. Nine and twelve hundredths _____
M. Sixteen hundredths _____	N. Eight and thirty-four hundredths _____
O. Seven and one tenth _____	P. Six and seventy-eight hundredths _____
Q. Eight tenths _____	R. Seven and ninety-one hundredths _____
S. Eight and sixty-three hundredths _____	T. One and eight hundredths _____

B	I	N	G	O
3.4	4.86	3.59	1.8	9.3
7.91	4.2	5.06	7.1	8.34
0.16	0.8	7.01	2.45	1.08
3.04	1.14	5.17	8.63	2.7
10.2	4.02	6.78	5.6	9.12

J331003 Clearly Math • Grade 3

Match Made in Heaven

Use a ruler to draw a straight line from each fraction to its matching decimal amount.

$\frac{8}{10}$

$\frac{3}{10}$ 0.03

$\frac{5}{100}$

0.08

0.09

0.05 •

0.5 •

• 0.8

$\frac{9}{10}$

0.3

0.9

$\frac{3}{100}$

$\frac{5}{10}$

$\frac{8}{100}$ $\frac{9}{100}$

What design did you make? _____

Shady Sums and Differences

Add or subtract. Shade sections with solutions greater than or equal to 5.5.

3.6 + 1.9	8.7 − 4.2	6.5 − 0.9	2.45 + 3.04	8.9 − 2.4
1.25 + 4.4	7.3 − 2.0	2.79 + 3.0	0.6 + 4.4	4.2 + 1.1
1.98 + 3.53	7.86 − 2.3	4.98 + 0.6	3.52 + 1.97	9.9 − 4.4
5.2 + 0.9	8.96 − 3.81	4.9 + 1.9	2.5 + 2.7	7.3 − 1.7
4.55 + 1.0	6.8 − 1.4	7.75 − 2.25	9.31 − 4.0	3.5 + 2.1

What word do you see? _____

Data and Probability

Beanbag Toss Predictions

Students will use logical reasoning and probability to determine the fairness of a game.

Blue 12 points	Orange 16 points	Yellow 18 points	Green 20 points	Red 24 points

1. Display the *Beanbag Game* transparency. Ask the students to quickly order the sizes of the sections from greatest to least (blue, orange, yellow, green, red).

2. Tell the students that in this game, they will choose one color. If they toss a counter and it lands on the color that they choose, they win. Challenge the students to decide if the game is fair and invite them to justify their responses. (Most students will say that the game is not fair because the sections are not equal in size.)

3. Call attention to the point values at the top of the transparency. Invite students to discuss in small groups whether the point value system makes the game fair. (Most students will think that the game is fair, since the largest point values are assigned to the smallest sections.)

4. As an extension, challenge the students to make gameboards that are fair for all players. Invite them to share their gameboards with the class and describe why they think they are fair.

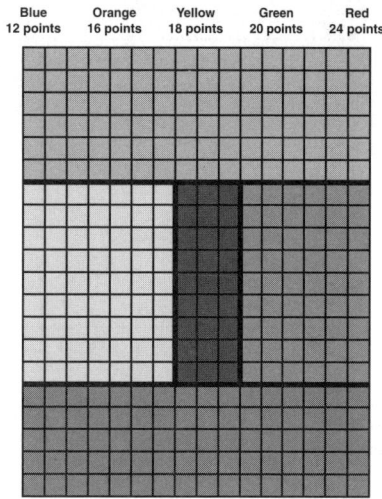

Survey and Analyze

In this activity, students will conduct a survey and analyze the results.

1. Have students work in small groups. Invite them to decide on a topic with which to survey their classmates. For example, students may collect data about their classmates' heights.

2. Ask student groups to decide how they would collect the data and organize it so that it could be shared with the class. Once the group has decided, allow time for the actual data collection. Then provide whatever supplies are necessary for the students to share the data.

3. Ask each student to write a paragraph describing his or her group's survey, how the group collected it, how the group displayed it, and what information the group got by analyzing it. The students' responses should be clear and complete. The students may include a sketch or some summary of the data that their groups displayed. Their analysis should reflect an understanding of the data and how it could be used. Perhaps they will interpret the data to make a decision or form an opinion.

Copycat Patterns

In this creative activity, students will follow and extend each other's patterns.

1. Show the students a pattern such as 2, 4, 6. Ask the students to name numbers that may come next. Invite creative responses. (For example, one response may be 10, since the sum of the first two numbers is the third number, and the sum of the next two numbers could be the fourth number.)

2. Have students work in pairs to create patterns of their own. Patterns may utilize numbers, shapes, sounds, or movements.

3. Allow the students time to share their patterns with the class, and invite the class to offer and justify possible numbers falling next in the sequence.

What's in a Name?

The pictograph shows the number of letters in students' first names.

Letters in Our First Names

3 or fewer letters	☺
4 letters	☺ ☺
5 letters	☺ ☺ ☺ ☺ ☺ ☺
6 letters	☺ ☺ ☺
7 or more letters	☺ ☺

Key: 1 ☺ = 5 students

Use the pictograph to answer the questions.

A. What does each symbol stand for? _____

B. How many students' first names contain 6 letters?_____

C. How many students' first names contain 4 letters?_____

D. How many letters long are 30 students' names?_____

E. How many students are shown on this pictograph?_____

F. How many more students have names with 4 letters than with 3 or fewer letters?

_____

G. Suppose 25 more students say they have 3 or fewer letters in their names. How would the pictograph change?

_____

_____

H. Write a question about the graph. Then answer the question.

_____

_____

Name _____

Be a Sport

The bar graph shows favorite sports of third grade students.

Our Favorite Sports

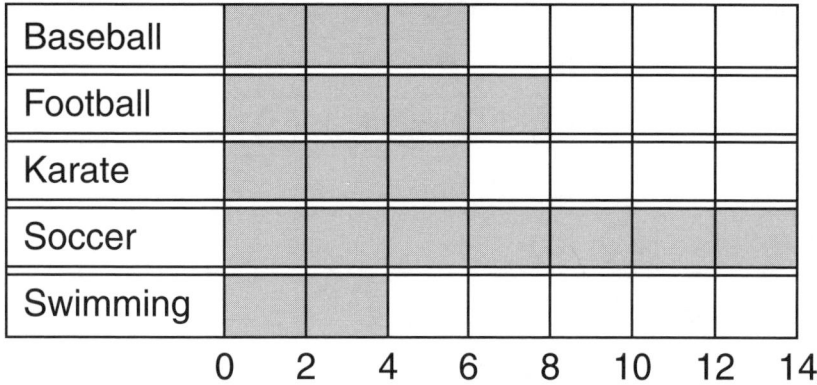

Baseball							
Football							
Karate							
Soccer							
Swimming							

0   2   4   6   8   10   12   14

Use the bar graph to answer the questions.

A. Which sport was chosen by 8 students?

_____

B. Which sport was chosen by 4 students?

_____

C. How many more students chose karate than swimming?

_____

D. Which two sports were chosen by the same number of students?

_____

E. Which sport was chosen by the greatest number of students? How many students chose it?

_____

F. How many more students would need to choose football in order for it to have the same number of votes as soccer?

_____

G. Write a question about the graph. Then answer the question.

_____

_____

Take a Chance

What is the probability that you will spin the numbers shown? The first problem has been done for you.

A.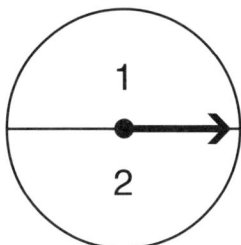

1: __1__ out of __2__

2: __1__ out of __2__

B.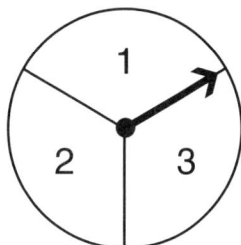

1: ___ out of ___

2: ___ out of ___

C.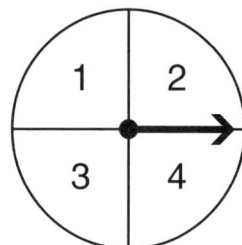

1: ___ out of ___

2: ___ out of ___

D.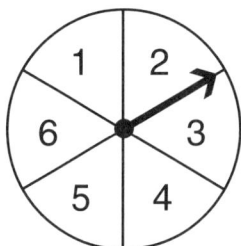

1: ___ out of ___

2: ___ out of ___

E.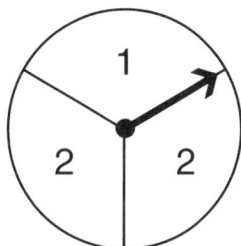

1: ___ out of ___

2: ___ out of ___

F.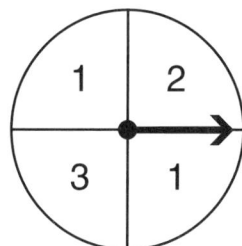

1: ___ out of ___

2: ___ out of ___

G.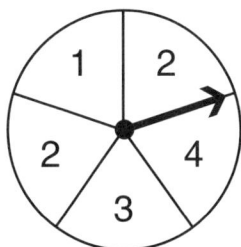

1: ___ out of ___

2: ___ out of ___

H.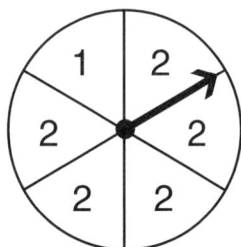

1: ___ out of ___

2: ___ out of ___

I.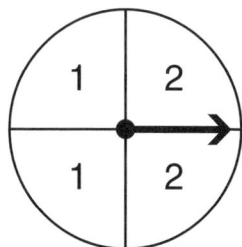

1: ___ out of ___

2: ___ out of ___

Answers

Page 6

Across

A.	3498	C.	1267
F.	135	H.	456
J.	8241	K.	894
L.	252	N.	32
P.	4237	R.	305
S.	903		

Down

A.	3508	B.	9314
D.	2049	E.	716
H.	3123	I.	5430
K.	82	M.	5734
O.	2590	P.	409
Q.	23	R.	391

A3	4	B9	8			C1	D2	6	E7
5		3				0			1
0		F1	G3	5		H4	5	6	
J8	2	4	1		K8	9	4		
			L2	M5	2		N3	O2	
	P4	Q2	3	7		R3	0	5	
S9	0	3		3		9		9	
		9		4		1		0	

Page 7

366	>	336	251	=	251	582	<	587
	blue			yellow			red	
672	<	678	805	>	795	780	<	870
	red			blue			red	
2,407	<	2,798	3,031	=	3,031	8,017	<	8,107
	red			yellow			red	
1,809	>	1,798	2,241	>	2,239	5,556	>	5,554
	blue			blue			blue	
1,011	<	1,100	1,101	=	1,101	1,486	<	1,488
	red			yellow			red	
1,247	>	989	8,023	<	9,154	1,057	>	1,009
	blue			red			blue	
7,957	<	8,012	5,468	=	5,468	2,034	>	1,999
	red			yellow			blue	

Red > blue > yellow.

Page 8

1.	743; O	2.	998; N
3.	897; E	4.	231; T
5.	802; H	6.	991; U
7.	9,165; S	8.	5,032; A
9.	7,914; D	10.	6,875; S
11.	8,795; V	12.	5,794; R
13.	4,190; I	14.	9,100; X
15.	7,910; Y		

About how many steps are taken to walk a mile: ONE THOUSAND SEVEN HUNDRED SIXTY

Page 9

A.	$0.75 change
B.	$0.61 change
C.	$0.45 change
D.	$0.33 change
E.	$0.27 change
F.	Yes
G.	Yes

Page 12

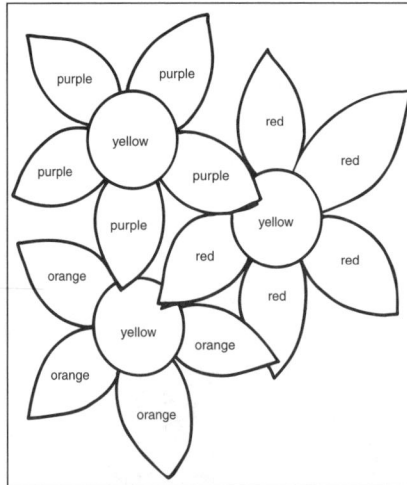

Describe the number patterns: Each flower has the same sum in the center and one sum for all the petals.

Page 13

A. $0.73 + $0.25 + $0.55 = $1.53

B. $1.75 + $0.67 + $0.39 = $2.81

C. $2.79 + $2.49 + $1.95 = $7.23

D. $4.75 + $2.59 + $0.39 = $7.73

E. $5.50 + $0.39 + $2.59 + $0.55 = $9.03

F. $1.95 + $3.25 + $2.49 + $0.73 = $8.42

G. Answers will vary.

H. Answers will vary but should indicate the use of estimation.

Page 14

A. 644, 233, 245, 367, 260

B. 346, 192, 718, 104, 547

C. 304, 703, 382, 452, 85

D. 450, 789, 371, 801, 598

M	A	T	H	O
450	192	382	200	85
644	789	598	452	346
703	718	400	245	304
600	371	233	547	300
104	500	260	367	801

Page 15

U.	1,346	O.	3,162
I.	2,658	I.	1,680
E.	503	E.	3,107
A.	4,088	C.	1,235
L.	1,225	L.	5,894
M.	2,428	M.	3,160
M.	5,181	N.	4,759
N.	1,515	P.	1,944
R.	5,745	S.	6,403
T.	2,057	Y.	2,814

One hundred years is a CENTURY

One thousand years is a MILLENNIUM

Page 16

A.	3,928	B.	4,999
C.	3,784	D.	2,998
E.	3,784	F.	3,784
G.	2,998	H.	4,929
I.	3,829	J.	2,929
K.	2,387	L.	4,999
M.	2,387	N.	4,929
O.	2,998	P.	5,211
Q.	Strategies will vary.		

Page 17

A. 125 − 92 = 33 more

B. 142 − 79 = 63 fewer

C. 79 + 96 + 83 = 258 students

D. 115 + 125 + 131 = 371 students

E. 96 + 118 = 214 students

F. 79 + 142 = 221 students

G. No; 72 + 92 + 84 + 79 + 96 + 83 = 506; 506 > 500.

H. Yes; 115 + 125 + 131 + 142 + 118 + 125 = 756; 756 < 800.

Page 21

1.	10; T	2.	20; U
3.	30; R	4.	45; N
5.	80; A	6.	18; R
7.	40; O	8.	16; U
9.	14; N	10.	70; D
11.	12; F	12.	35; A
13.	60; C	14.	25; T
15.	100; S		

16. Pairs of multiplication sentences are called TURNAROUND FACTS.

6 x 9 = 54 blue	4 x 7 = 28 green	3 x 7 = 21 yellow	3 x 10 = 30 green	6 x 8 = 48 blue
4 x 10 = 40 green	3 x 4 = 12 yellow	3 x 8 = 24 yellow	4 x 4 = 16 yellow	6 x 5 = 30 green
6 x 3 = 18 yellow	3 x 2 = 6 red	4 x 1 = 4 red	3 x 3 = 9 red	3 x 6 = 18 yellow
6 x 4 = 24 yellow	6 x 1 = 6 red	4 x 2 = 8 red	3 x 1 = 3 red	6 x 2 = 12 yellow
4 x 9 = 36 green	4 x 3 = 12 yellow	4 x 6 = 24 yellow	3 x 5 = 15 yellow	4 x 8 = 32 green
6 x 10 = 60 blue	3 x 9 = 27 green	4 x 5 = 20 yellow	6 x 6 = 36 green	6 x 7 = 42 blue

What do you notice about every blue section? One of the factors is 6.

Page 23

A. T: 7 x 3 = 21; F: 8 x 5 ≠ 41 (40); T: 9 x 3 = 27

B. T: 7 x 0 = 0; F: 9 x 7 ≠ 67 (63); F: 7 x 7 ≠ 51 (49)

C. F: 9 x 2 ≠ 19 (18); T: 7 x 2 = 14; F: 8 x 2 ≠ 17 (16)

D. T: 8 x 9 = 72; F: 7 x 4 ≠ 29 (28); T: 8 x 0 = 0

E. F: 9 x 6 ≠ 53 (54); T: 8 x 10 = 80; F: 7 x 5 ≠ 37 (35)

F. F: 7 x 6 ≠ 43 (42); F: 9 x 8 ≠ 73 (72); T: 9 x 5 = 45

G. F: 7 x 7 ≠ 47 (49); F: 8 x 7 ≠ 57 (56); F: 8 x 4 ≠ 33 (32)

H. F: 9 x 0 ≠ 9 (0); F: 9 x 9 ≠ 83 (81); F: 9 x 10 ≠ 19 (90)

I. T: 8 x 8 = 64; T: 9 x 4 = 36; F: 8 x 3 ≠ 23 (24)

J. T: 7 x 8 = 56; F: 8 x 6 ≠ 47 (48); F: 7 x 9 ≠ 69 (63)

True statements < false statements.

Page 24

Page 25

A. Samantha: 4 x 12 = 48
   Kyle: 3 x 18 = 54
   Kyle won the game.

B. Ronni: 4 x 16 = 64
   Mike: 3 x 20 = 60
   Ronni won the game.

C. Jessica: 3 x 12 = 36
   Adam: 2 x 18 = 36
   Jessica and Adam tied.

D. Ruth: 5 x 12 = 60
   Gene: 4 x 18 = 72
   Gene won the game.

E. Sam: 4 x 24 = 96
   Annie: 5 x 18 = 90
   Sam won the game.

F. Ethel: 4 x 12 = 48
   Dave: 3 x 16 = 48
   Ethel and Dave tied.

Page 28

18 ÷ 2 = 9	14 ÷ 2 = 7	16 ÷ 4 = 4
16 ÷ 2 = 8	20 ÷ 4 = 5	10 ÷ 2 = 5
8 ÷ 4 = ~~4~~ = 2	21 ÷ 3 = 7	12 ÷ 2 = ~~5~~ = 6
28 ÷ 4 = ~~8~~ = 7	32 ÷ 4 = 8	12 ÷ 3 = ~~3~~ = 4
6 ÷ 2 = ~~4~~ = 3	24 ÷ 4 = 6	4 ÷ 4 = ~~0~~ = 1
2 ÷ 2 = ~~0~~ = 1	36 ÷ 4 = 9	8 ÷ 2 = ~~6~~ = 4
24 ÷ 3 = ~~7~~ = 8	18 ÷ 3 = 6	4 ÷ 2 = ~~1~~ = 2
6 ÷ 3 = ~~3~~ = 2	12 ÷ 4 = 3	15 ÷ 3 = ~~12~~ = 5
3 ÷ 3 = ~~0~~ = 1	30 ÷ 3 = 10	9 ÷ 3 = ~~6~~ = 3
20 ÷ 2 = ~~2~~ = 10	27 ÷ 3 = 9	40 ÷ 4 = ~~12~~ = 10

The yellow sections form the letter *T*.

Page 29

1	4 ÷ 4	5 ÷ 5	6 ÷ 6	~~X~~ ÷ 7 = 7
2	8 ÷ 4	10 ÷ 5	~~X~~ ÷ 6 = 12	14 ÷ 7
3	12 ÷ 4	~~X~~ ÷ 5 = 15	18 ÷ 6	21 ÷ 7
4	~~X~~ ÷ 4 = 16	20 ÷ 5	24 ÷ 6	28 ÷ 7
5	20 ÷ 4	~~X~~ ÷ 5 = 25	30 ÷ 6	35 ÷ 7
6	24 ÷ 4	30 ÷ 5	~~X~~ ÷ 6 = 36	42 ÷ 7
7	28 ÷ 4	35 ÷ 5	42 ÷ 6	~~X~~ ÷ 7 = 49
8	32 ÷ 4	40 ÷ 5	~~X~~ ÷ 6 = 48	56 ÷ 7
9	36 ÷ 4	~~X~~ ÷ 5 = 45	54 ÷ 6	63 ÷ 7
10	~~X~~ ÷ 4 = 40	50 ÷ 5	60 ÷ 6	70 ÷ 7

Page 30

1. 9; P
2. 7; I
3. 8; C
4. 7; N
5. 8; I
6. 7; C
7. 8; T
8. 9; A
9. 8; B
10. 9; L
11. 7; E

What has 4 legs and flies? A PICNIC TABLE

Page 31

4 x 7 = 28 yellow	56 ÷ 8 = 7 green	6 x 8 = 48 red	45 ÷ 5 = 9 orange
6 x 7 = 42 purple	28 ÷ 7 = 4 yellow	48 ÷ 8 = 6 red	9 x 5 = 45 orange
72 ÷ 9 = 8 blue	42 ÷ 7 = 6 purple	28 ÷ 4 = 7 yellow	8 x 7 = 56 green
56 ÷ 7 = 8 green	9 x 8 = 72 blue	7 x 6 = 42 purple	7 x 4 = 28 yellow
5 x 9 = 45 orange	8 x 6 = 48 red	72 ÷ 8 = 9 blue	42 ÷ 6 = 7 purple
45 ÷ 9 = 5 orange	48 ÷ 6 = 8 red	7 x 8 = 56 green	8 x 9 = 72 blue

Fact families:
   8, 64; 8 x 8 = 64, 64 ÷ 8 = 8
   7, 49; 7 x 7 = 49, 49 ÷ 7 = 7
   9, 81; 9 x 9 = 81, 81 ÷ 9 = 9
   6, 36; 6 x 6 = 36, 36 ÷ 6 = 6

How are these families different from the color table above? Two of their factors are the same, so there are only two facts in the family.

Page 32

A. Rule: Divide by 5
   Out: 1, 2, **3**, **4**, **5**, **6**, **7**, **8**, **9**, **10**

B. Rule: Divide by 2
   Out: 10, 9, **8**, **7**, **6**, **5**, **4**, **3**, **2**, **1**

C. Rule: Divide by 3
   Out: 6, **5**, 7, **3**, 1, **10**, **2**, **4**, **8**, **9**

D. Rule: Divide by 9
   Out: 10, 1, **9**, 2, **8**, 3, **7**, **4**, **6**, **5**

E. Rule: Divide by 4
   Out: **5**, 10, **3**, 8, 1, **6**, **4**, **9**, **2**, 7

F. Rule: Divide by 8
   Out: 10, 5, **9**, 4, **8**, 3, **7**, **2**, **6**, 1

Page 33

A. 72 ÷ 3 = 24 students

B. 92 ÷ 4 = 23 students

C. 84 ÷ 3 = 28 students

D. 96 ÷ 4 = 24 students

E. 79 ÷ 3 = 26 R1. There are 26 in two classes; 27 in the third class.

F. 83 ÷ 3 = 27 R2. There are 28 in two classes; 27 in the third class.

G. 3 + 4 + 3 + 4 + 3 + 3 = 20 classes

Page 37
A. Perimeter = 22 inches
B. Perimeter = 18 inches
C. Perimeter = 14 inches
D. Perimeter = 10 inches
E. Answers will vary.

Page 38
A. About 5 cm   B. About 8 cm
C. About 12 cm   D. About 4 cm
E. About 10 cm   F. About 3 cm
G. About 11 cm
H. Lines should be between 6.5 and 7.4 centimeters long.
I. B, the orange pencil.

Page 39
K. Area = 28 square units
D. Area = 48 square units
E. Area = 20 square units
A. Area = 18 square units
N. Area = 24 square units
O. Area = 27 square units
Y. Area = 80 square units

What is the most difficult key to turn? A DONKEY

Page 40
C. 11:09   E. 8:42
F. 10:23   H. 9:02
I. 3:21   K. 3:58
L. 2:34   M. 4:13
O. 6:48   S. 4:20
T. 12:12   X. 9:39

What time is it when the clock strikes 13? TIME TO FIX THE CLOCK

Page 41
1. 9:00   2. 1:30
3. 6:15   4. 3:40
5. 4:00   6. 7:30

Page 44

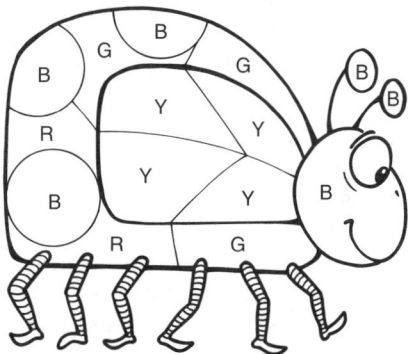

What pattern do you see in the numerators and denominators? The denominator is always twice as great as the numerator.

Page 45
1. $1/2$; T   2. $3/4$; H
3. $1/2$; E   4. $3/8$; Y
5. $5/8$; N   6. $3/4$; V
7. $2/3$; R   8. $7/8$; S
9. $2/3$; O

Why can't hurricanes get along? THEY NEVER SEE EYE TO EYE

Page 46

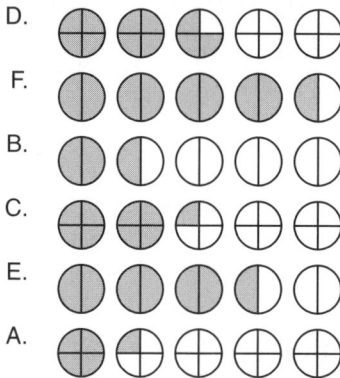

What pattern do you notice? The letters are in alphabetical order.

Page 47
A. 3.4   B. 4.2
C. 5.17   D. 2.45
E. 9.3   F. 10.2
G. 1.14   H. 5.6
I. 2.7   J. 3.59
K. 4.86   L. 9.12
M. 0.16   N. 8.34
O. 7.1   P. 6.78
Q. 0.8   R. 7.91
S. 8.63   T. 1.08

B	I	N	G	O
3.4	4.86	3.59	1.8	9.3
7.91	4.2	5.06	7.1	8.34
0.16	0.8	7.01	2.45	1.08
3.04	1.14	5.17	8.63	2.7
10.2	4.02	6.78	5.6	9.12

Page 48

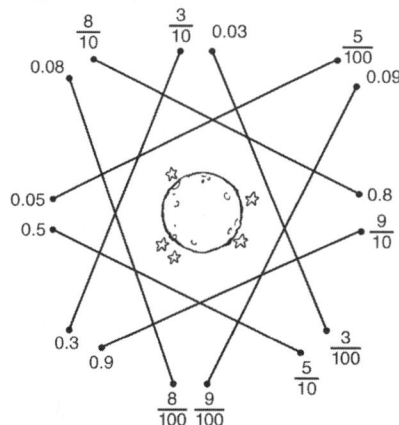

What design was made? A star.

Page 49

3.6 + 1.9 5.5	8.7 − 4.2 4.5	6.5 − 0.9 5.6	2.45 + 3.04 5.49	8.9 − 2.4 6.5
1.25 + 4.4 5.65	7.3 − 2.0 5.3	2.79 + 3.0 5.79	0.6 + 4.4 5.0	4.2 + 1.1 5.3
1.98 + 3.53 5.51	7.86 − 2.3 5.56	4.98 + 0.6 5.58	3.52 + 1.97 5.49	9.9 − 4.4 5.5
5.2 + 0.9 6.1	8.96 − 3.81 5.15	4.9 + 1.9 6.8	2.5 + 2.7 5.2	7.3 − 1.7 5.6
4.55 + 1.0 5.55	6.8 − 1.4 5.4	7.75 − 2.25 5.50	9.31 − 4.0 5.31	3.5 + 2.1 5.6

What word do you see? *Hi.*

Page 51
A 5 students   B. 15 students
C. 10 students   D. 5 letters
E. 70 students   F. 5 students
G. Another five symbols would be added to the "3 or fewer letters" category, bringing the total amount to 30 students
H. Questions and answers will vary.

Page 52
A. Football
B. Swimming
C. 2 more students
D. Karate and baseball
E. Soccer; 14 students
F. 6 students
G. Answers will vary.

Page 53
A. 1: 1 out of 2; 2:1 out of 2
B. 1: 1 out of 3; 2: 1 out of 3
C. 1: 1 out of 4; 2: 1 out of 4
D. 1: 1 out of 6; 2: 1 out of 6
E. 1: 1 out of 3; 2: 2 out of 3
F. 1: 2 out of 4; 2: 1 out of 4
G. 1: 1 out of 5; 2: 2 out of 5
H. 1: 1 out of 6; 2: 5 out of 6
I. 1: 2 out of 4; 2: 2 out of 4
J. Answers will vary.